Bilingual
VISUAL
dictionary

Bilingual

VISUAL

dictionary

Previously published as part of
5-Language Visual Dictionary

Penguin
Random
House

DK LONDON
Senior Editors Angeles Gavira, Christine Stroyan, Angela Wilkes
Senior Art Editor Ina Stradins
Jacket Editor Claire Gell
Jacket Design Development Manager Sophia MTT
Preproduction Producer Andy Hilliard
Producer Jude Crozier
Picture Researcher Anna Grapes
Managing Editor Dan Mills
Managing Art Editors Anna Hall, Phil Ormerod
Associate Publisher Liz Wheeler
Publisher Jonathan Metcalf

DK INDIA
Editors Arpita Dasgupta, Shreya Sengupta, Arani Sinha
Assistant Editors Sugandha Agarwal, Priyanjali Narain
DTP Designers Harish Aggarwal, Ashwani Tyagi, Anita Yadav
Jacket Designer Juhi Sheth
Managing Jacket Editor Saloni Singh
Preproduction Manager Balwant Singh
Production Manager Pankaj Sharma

Designed for DK by WaltonCreative.com
Art Editor Colin Walton, assisted by Tracy Musson
Designers Peter Radcliffe, Earl Neish, Ann Cannings
Picture Research Marissa Keating

Language content for DK by g-and-w PUBLISHING
Managed by Jane Wightwick, assisted by Ana Bremón
Translation and editing by Christine Arthur
Additional input by Dr. Arturo Pretel, Martin Prill,
Frédéric Monteil, Meinrad Prill, Mari Bremón, Oscar Bremón,
Anunchi Bremón, Leila Gaafar

First American Edition, 2009
This edition published in the United States in 2017 by DK
Publishing, 345 Hudson Street, New York, New York 10014

Copyright © 2009, 2015, 2017 Dorling Kindersley Limited
DK, a Division of Penguin Random House LLC
17 18 19 20 21 10 9 8 7 6 5 4 3 2 1
001—306409—Apr/17

A catalog record for this book is available
from the Library of Congress.
ISBN: 978-1-4654-5931-2

DK books are available at special discounts when purchased
in bulk for sales promotions, premiums, fund-raising, or
educational use. For details, contact: DK Publishing Special
Markets, 345 Hudson Street, New York, New York 10014
SpecialSales@dk.com

Printed and bound in China

A WORLD OF IDEAS:
SEE ALL THERE IS TO KNOW

www.dk.com

contenido
contents

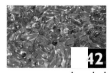

la gente • people

el aspecto • appearance

la salud • health

la casa • home

los servicios • services

las compras • shopping

los alimentos • food

sobre el diccionario

Está comprobado que el empleo de fotografías ayuda a la comprensión y a la retención de información. Basados en este principio, este diccionario bilingüe y altamente ilustrado exhibe un amplio registro de vocabulario útil y actual en dos idiomas europeos.

El diccionario aparece dividido según su temática y abarca la mayoría de los aspectos del mundo cotidiano con detalle, desde el restaurante al gimnasio, la casa al lugar de trabajo, el espacio al reino animal. Encontrará también palabras y frases adicionales para su uso en conversación y para ampliar su vocabulario.

Este diccionario es un instrumento de referencia esencial para todo aquél que esté interesado en los idiomas; es práctico, estimulante y fácil de usar.

Algunos puntos a observar

Los dos idiomas se presentan siempre en el mismo orden: español (mejicano y castellano) e inglés. Cuando existen diferencias entre el castellano y el español mejicano, el mejicano aparece primero seguido por el castellano; este último entre paréntesis e indicado con una ^C: **la llave** (^C **el grifo**).

En español, los sustantivos se muestran con sus artículos definidos reflejando el género (masculino o femenino) y el número (singular/plural):

la semilla	**las almendras**
seed	almonds

Los verbos se indican con una (v) después del inglés:

recolectar • harvest (v)

Cada idioma tiene su propio índice. Aquí podrá mirar una palabra en cualquiera de los dos idiomas y se le indicará el número de la página donde aparece. El género se indica utilizando las siguientes abreviaturas:

m = masculino   f = femenino

cómo utilizar este libro

Ya se encuentre aprendiendo un idioma nuevo por motivos de trabajo, placer, o para preparar sus vacaciones al extranjero, o ya quiera ampliar su vocabulario en un idioma que ya conoce, este diccionario es un instrumento muy valioso que podrá utilizar de distintas maneras.

Cuando esté aprendiendo un idioma nuevo, busque palabras similares en distintos idiomas y palabras que parecen similares pero que poseen significados totalmente distintos. También podrá observar cómo los idiomas se influyen unos a otros. Por ejemplo, la lengua inglesa ha importado muchos términos de comida de otras lenguas pero, a cambio, ha exportado términos empleados en tecnología y cultura popular.

Actividades prácticas de aprendizaje

• Mientras se desplaza por su casa, lugar de trabajo o colegio, intente mirar las páginas que se refieren a ese lugar. Podrá entonces cerrar el libro, mirar a su alrededor y ver cuántos objetos o características puede nombrar.

• Desafíese a usted mismo a escribir una historia, carta o diálogo empleando tantos términos de una página concreta como le sea posible. Esto le ayudará a retener vocabulario y recordar la ortografía. Si quiere ir progresando para poder escribir un texto más largo, comience con frases que incorporen 2 ó 3 palabras.

• Si tiene buena memoria visual, intente dibujar o calcar objetos del libro; luego cierre el libro y escriba las palabras correspondientes debajo del dibujo.

• Cuando se sienta más seguro, escoja palabras del índice de uno de los idiomas y vea si sabe lo que significan antes de consultar la página correspondiente para comprobarlo.

app de audio gratuita

Esta app de audio incluye todas las palabras y frases del libro, leídas por hablantes nativos tanto de (el idioma) como de inglés, para facilitar el aprendizaje de vocabulario importante y mejorar la pronunciación.

cómo utilizar la app de audio

• Descargar la app gratuita en el teléfono o tableta desde la tienda elegida
• Abrir la aplicación para desbloquear el Diccionario Visual correspondiente en la Biblioteca.
• Descargar los archivos de audio del libro.
• Introducir el número de página, desplazar la lista de arriba a abajo para encontrar la palabra o frase.
• Pulsar sobre una palabra para escucharla.
• Pulsar a izquierda o derecha para ver la página anterior y siguiente.

Nota

En el libro hay casos en los que además de la versión mexicana de la palabra aparece una alternativa de español de España, sin embargo en la app aparece únicamente la versión mexicana.

about the dictionary

The use of pictures is proven to aid understanding and the retention of information. Working on this principle, this highly illustrated bilingual dictionary presents a large range of useful current vocabulary in two European languages.

The dictionary is divided thematically and covers most aspects of the everyday world in detail, from the restaurant to the gym, the home to the workplace, outer space to the animal kingdom. You will also find additional words and phrases for conversational use and for extending your vocabulary.

This is an essential reference tool for anyone interested in languages—practical, stimulating, and easy-to-use.

A few things to note

The two languages are always presented in the same order—Spanish (Mexican and Castilian) and English. Where a word or phrase is different in Castilian and Mexican Spanish, the Mexican appears first, followed by the Castilian; the latter in brackets and indicated by a ^{C}: la **llave** (^{C}**el grifo**).

In Spanish, nouns are given with their definite articles reflecting the gender (masculine or feminine) and number (singular or plural), for example:

la semilla   **las almendras**
seed   almonds

Verbs are indicated by a (v) after the English, for example:

recolectar • harvest (v)

Each language also has its own index at the back of the book. Here you can look up a word in either of the two languages and be referred to the page number(s) where it appears. The gender is shown using the following abbreviations:

m = masculine   f = feminine

how to use this book

Whether you are learning a new language for business, pleasure, or in preparation for an overseas vacation, or are hoping to extend your vocabulary in an already familiar language, this dictionary is a valuable learning tool that you can use in a number of different ways.

When learning a new language, look for cognates (words that are alike in different languages) and "false friends" (words that look alike but carry significantly different meanings). You can also see where the languages have influenced each other. For example, English has imported many terms for food from other European languages but, in turn, exported terms used in technology and popular culture.

Practical learning activities

• As you move around your home, workplace, or school, try looking at the pages which cover that setting. You could then close the book, look around you, and see how many of the objects and features you can name.
• Challenge yourself to write a story, letter, or dialogue using as many of the terms on a particular page as possible. This will help you retain the vocabulary and remember the spelling. If you want to build up to writing a longer text, start with sentences incorporating 2–3 words.
• If you have a very visual memory, try drawing or tracing items from the book onto a piece of paper, then closing the book and filling in the words below the picture.
• Once you are more confident, pick out words in a foreign-language index and see if you know what they mean before turning to the relevant page to see if you were right.

free audio app

The audio app contains all the words and phrases in the book, spoken by native speakers in both Spanish and English, making it easier to learn important vocabulary and improve your pronunciation.

how to use the audio app

• Download the free app on your smartphone or tablet from your chosen app store.
• Open the app and unlock your *Visual Dictionary* in the Library.
• Download the audio files for your book.
• Enter a page number, then scroll up and down through the list to find a word or phrase.
• Tap a word to hear it.
• Swipe left or right to view the previous or next page.

A note about Mexican and Castilian Spanish

Where an alternative Castilian version of a Mexican word is given in the book, only the Mexican Spanish translation is given in the app.

la gente
people

el cuerpo • body

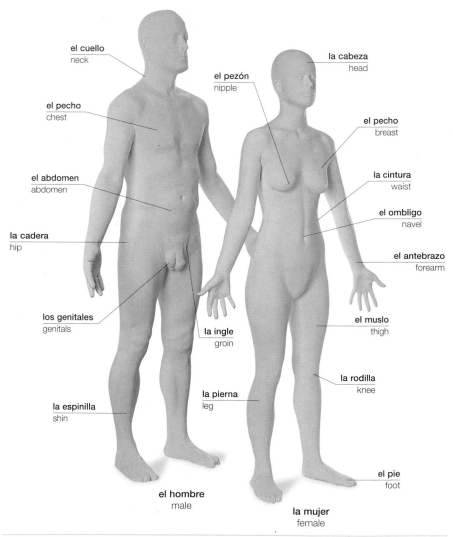

el cuello
neck

la cabeza
head

el pezón
nipple

el pecho
chest

el pecho
breast

la cintura
waist

el abdomen
abdomen

el ombligo
navel

la cadera
hip

el antebrazo
forearm

los genitales
genitals

la ingle
groin

el muslo
thigh

la rodilla
knee

la espinilla
shin

la pierna
leg

el pie
foot

el hombre
male

la mujer
female

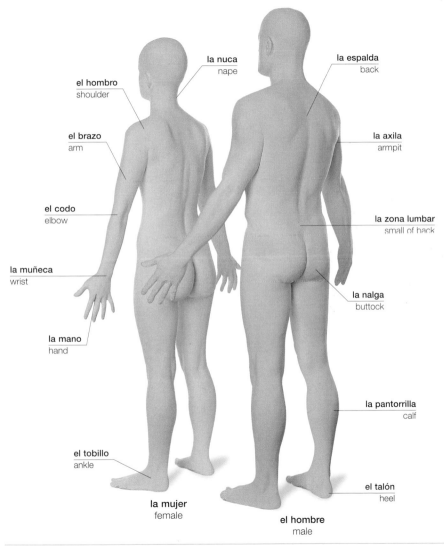

la nuca
nape

la espalda
back

el hombro
shoulder

el brazo
arm

la axila
armpit

el codo
elbow

la zona lumbar
small of back

la muñeca
wrist

la nalga
buttock

la mano
hand

la pantorrilla
calf

el tobillo
ankle

el talón
heel

la mujer
female

el hombre
male

la cara • face

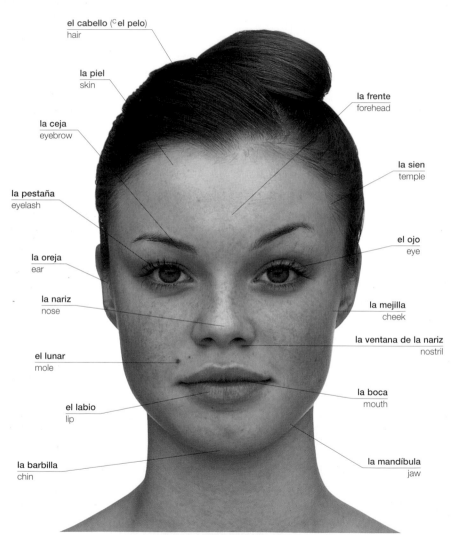

el cabello (^C el pelo)
hair

la piel
skin

la frente
forehead

la ceja
eyebrow

la sien
temple

la pestaña
eyelash

el ojo
eye

la oreja
ear

la mejilla
cheek

la nariz
nose

la ventana de la nariz
nostril

el lunar
mole

la boca
mouth

el labio
lip

la barbilla
chin

la mandíbula
jaw

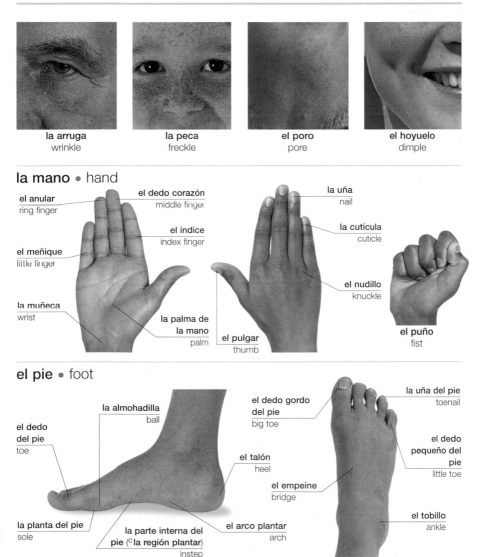

la arruga
wrinkle

la peca
freckle

el poro
pore

el hoyuelo
dimple

la mano • hand

el anular
ring finger

el dedo corazón
middle finger

el índice
index finger

el meñique
little finger

la muñeca
wrist

**la palma de
la mano**
palm

la uña
nail

la cutícula
cuticle

el nudillo
knuckle

el pulgar
thumb

el puño
fist

el pie • foot

la almohadilla
ball

**el dedo
del pie**
toe

la planta del pie
sole

**la parte interna del
pie (ᶜla región plantar)**
instep

**el dedo gordo
del pie**
big toe

el talón
heel

el empeine
bridge

el arco plantar
arch

la uña del pie
toenail

**el dedo
pequeño del
pie**
little toe

el tobillo
ankle

los músculos • muscles

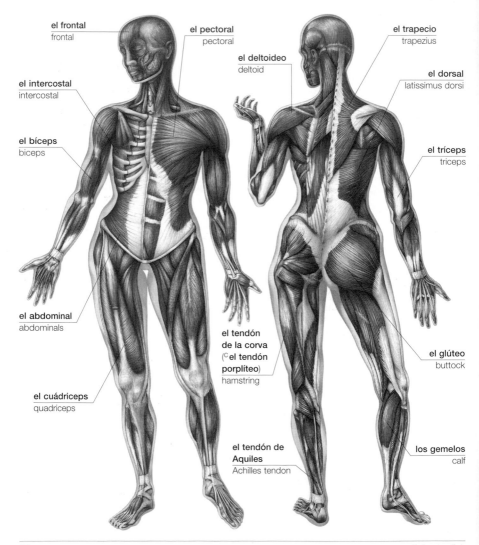

el frontal
frontal

el pectoral
pectoral

el deltoideo
deltoid

el trapecio
trapezius

el intercostal
intercostal

el dorsal
latissimus dorsi

el bíceps
biceps

el tríceps
triceps

el abdominal
abdominals

el tendón
de la corva
(ᶜ el tendón
porplíteo)
hamstring

el glúteo
buttock

el cuádriceps
quadriceps

el tendón de
Aquiles
Achilles tendon

los gemelos
calf

el esqueleto • skeleton

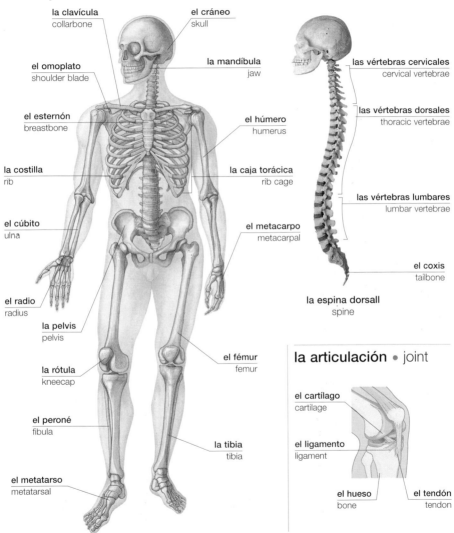

la clavícula
collarbone

el cráneo
skull

la mandíbula
jaw

el omoplato
shoulder blade

el esternón
breastbone

el húmero
humerus

la costilla
rib

la caja torácica
rib cage

el cúbito
ulna

el metacarpo
metacarpal

el radio
radius

la pelvis
pelvis

la rótula
kneecap

el fémur
femur

el peroné
fibula

la tibia
tibia

el metatarso
metatarsal

las vértebras cervicales
cervical vertebrae

las vértebras dorsales
thoracic vertebrae

las vértebras lumbares
lumbar vertebrae

el coxis
tailbone

la espina dorsall
spine

la articulación • joint

el cartílago
cartilage

el ligamento
ligament

el hueso
bone

el tendón
tendon

los órganos internos • internal organs

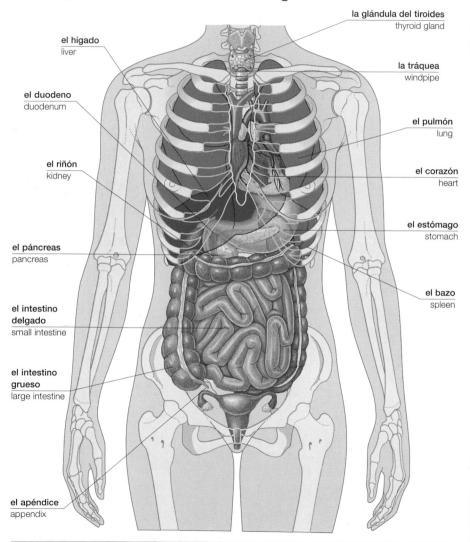

la glándula del tiroides
thyroid gland

el hígado
liver

el duodeno
duodenum

el riñón
kidney

el páncreas
pancreas

el intestino
delgado
small intestine

el intestino
grueso
large intestine

el apéndice
appendix

la tráquea
windpipe

el pulmón
lung

el corazón
heart

el estómago
stomach

el bazo
spleen

la cabeza • head

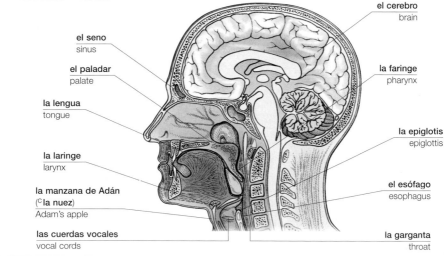

el cerebro
brain

el seno
sinus

el paladar
palate

la faringe
pharynx

la lengua
tongue

la epiglotis
epiglottis

la laringe
larynx

la manzana de Adán
(^Cla nuez)
Adam's apple

el esófago
esophagus

las cuerdas vocales
vocal cords

la garganta
throat

los sistemas • body systems

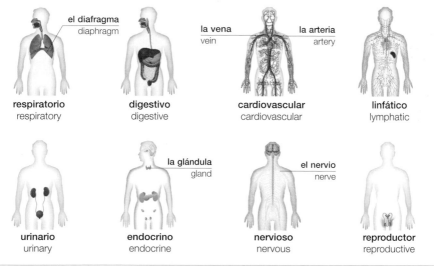

el diafragma
diaphragm

la vena
vein

la arteria
artery

respiratorio
respiratory

digestivo
digestive

cardiovascular
cardiovascular

linfático
lymphatic

la glándula
gland

el nervio
nerve

urinario
urinary

endocrino
endocrine

nervioso
nervous

reproductor
reproductive

los órganos reproductores • reproductive organs

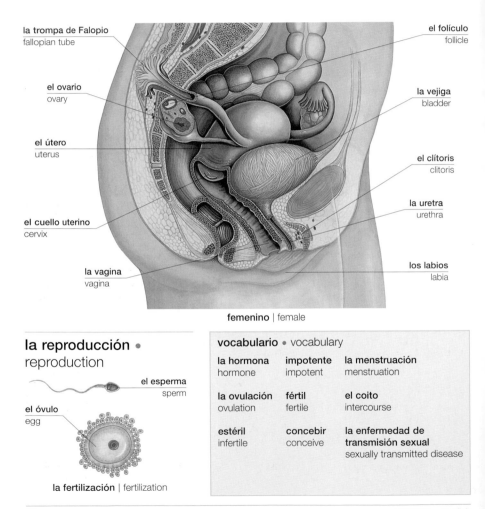

la trompa de Falopio
fallopian tube

el folículo
follicle

el ovario
ovary

la vejiga
bladder

el útero
uterus

el clítoris
clitoris

la uretra
urethra

el cuello uterino
cervix

la vagina
vagina

los labios
labia

femenino | female

la reproducción • reproduction

el esperma
sperm

el óvulo
egg

la fertilización | fertilization

vocabulario • vocabulary

la hormona hormone	impotente impotent	la menstruación menstruation
la ovulación ovulation	fértil fertile	el coito intercourse
estéril infertile	concebir conceive	la enfermedad de transmisión sexual sexually transmitted disease

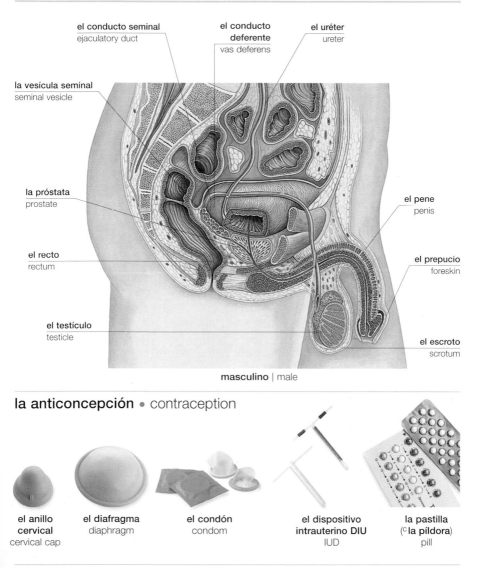

el conducto seminal
ejaculatory duct

el conducto
deferente
vas deferens

el uréter
ureter

la vesícula seminal
seminal vesicle

la próstata
prostate

el pene
penis

el recto
rectum

el prepucio
foreskin

el testículo
testicle

el escroto
scrotum

masculino | male

la anticoncepción • contraception

**el anillo
cervical**
cervical cap

el diafragma
diaphragm

el condón
condom

**el dispositivo
intrauterino DIU**
IUD

la pastilla
(ᶜ la píldora)
pill

la familia • family

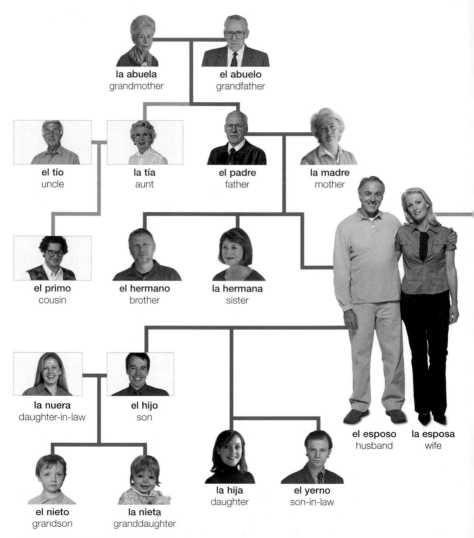

la abuela
grandmother

el abuelo
grandfather

el tío
uncle

la tía
aunt

el padre
father

la madre
mother

el primo
cousin

el hermano
brother

la hermana
sister

la nuera
daughter-in-law

el hijo
son

el esposo
husband

la esposa
wife

el nieto
grandson

la nieta
granddaughter

la hija
daughter

el yerno
son-in-law

vocabulario • vocabulary

los parientes relatives	**los padres** parents	**los nietos** grandchildren	**la madrastra** stepmother	**el hijastro** stepson	**la generación** generation
los abuelos grandparents	**los niños** children	**el padrastro** stepfather	**la hijastra** stepdaughter	**el/la compañero/-a** partner	**los gemelos** twins

la suegra
mother-in-law

el suegro
father-in-law

el cuñado
brother-in-law

la cuñada
sister-in-law

la sobrina
niece

el sobrino
nephew

los tratamientos •
titles

Señora
Mrs.

Señor
Mr.

Señorita
Miss/Ms.

las etapas • stages

el bebé
baby

el niño
child

el niño
boy

la niña
girl

la adolescente
teenager

el adulto
adult

el hombre
man

la mujer
woman

las relaciones • relationships

la asistente (ᶜ la ayudante)
assistant

el jefe
manager

la socia
business partner

el empresario
employer

la empleada
employee

el compañero
colleague

la oficina | office

la vecina
neighbor

el amigo
friend

el conocido
acquaintance

el amigo por correspondencia
pen pal

el novio
boyfriend

la novia
girlfriend

el prometido
fiancé

la prometida
fiancée

la pareja prometida | couple

la pareja | engaged couple

24

las emociones • emotions

la sonrisa
smile

contenta
happy

triste
sad

entusiasmada
excited

aburrido
bored

sorprendido
surprised

asustada
scared

el ceño
fruncido
frown

enfadada
angry

confundida
confused

preocupada
worried

nerviosa
nervous

orgullosos
proud

segura de sí misma
confident

avergonzada
embarrassed

tímida
shy

vocabulario • vocabulary

triste upset	**reír** laugh (v)	**suspirar** sigh (v)	**gritar** shout (v)
horrorizado shocked	**llorar** cry (v)	**desmayarse** faint (v)	**bostezar** yawn (v)

los acontecimientos de una vida • life events

nacer
be born (v)

empezar el colegio
start school (v)

hacer amigos
make friends (v)

graduarse (ᶜlicenciarse)
graduate (v)

conseguir un trabajo
get a job (v)

enamorarse
fall in love (v)

casarse
get married (v)

tener un hijo
have a baby (v)

la boda | wedding

el divorcio
divorce

el funeral
funeral

vocabulario • vocabulary

el bautizo
christening

el bar mitzvah
bar mitzvah

el aniversario
anniversary

emigrar
emigrate (v)

jubilarse
retire (v)

morir
die (v)

hacer testamento
make a will (v)

**la celebración
de la boda**
wedding reception

la luna de miel
honeymoon

el acta (ᶜla partida)
de nacimiento
birth certificate

las celebraciones • celebrations

la fiesta de cumpleaños
birthday party

la tarjeta
card

el cumpleaños
birthday

el regalo
present

la Navidad
Christmas

el Año Nuevo
New Year

el carnaval
carnival

el desfile
procession

la cinta
ribbon

el día de Acción de Gracias
Thanksgiving

la Pascua (ᶜla Semana Santa)
Easter

el día de Halloween
Halloween

los festivales • festivals

la Pascua judía
Passover

el Ramadán
Ramadan

el Diwali
Diwali

el aspecto
appearance

la ropa de niño • children's clothing

el bebé • baby

el traje de invierno (^C**el buzo**)
snowsuit

la camiseta
(^C**el body**)
bodysuit

el botón (^C**el corchete**)
snap

el mameluco
(^C**el pelele con pies**)
onesie

el mameluco
(^C**el pijama enterizo**)
sleeper

el mameluco (^C**el pelele**) **sin pies**
romper

el babero
bib

los guantes
(^C**los manoplas**)
mittens

las botas
(^C**los patucos**)
booties

el pañal de felpa
cloth diaper

**el pañal
desechable**
disposable diaper

el calzón (^C**las bra-
guitas**) **de plástico**
plastic pants

---

el niño pequeño • toddler

la playera
(^C**la camiseta**)
T-shirt

**los panatalones
con peto**
overalls

el gorro para el sol
sun hat

los shorts
(^C**los pantalones
cortos**)
shorts

la falda
skirt

el delantal
apron

el niño • child

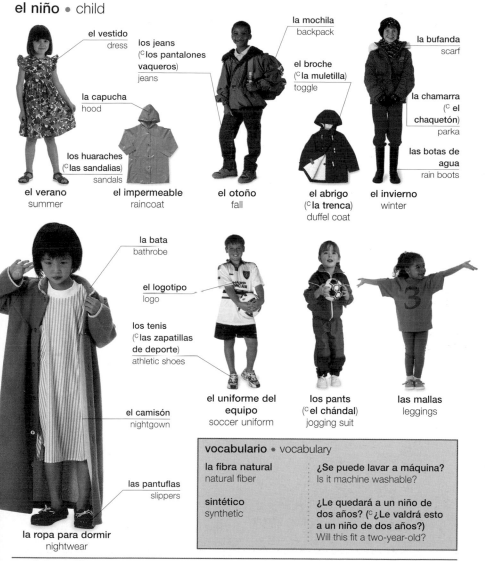

el vestido
dress

los jeans
(ᶜlos pantalones vaqueros)
jeans

la capucha
hood

los huaraches
(ᶜlas sandalias)
sandals

el verano
summer

el impermeable
raincoat

la mochila
backpack

el broche
(ᶜla muletilla)
toggle

el otoño
fall

el abrigo
(ᶜla trenca)
duffel coat

la bufanda
scarf

la chamarra
(ᶜ el chaquetón)
parka

las botas de agua
rain boots

el invierno
winter

la bata
bathrobe

el logotipo
logo

los tenis
(ᶜlas zapatillas de deporte)
athletic shoes

el camisón
nightgown

las pantuflas
slippers

la ropa para dormir
nightwear

el uniforme del equipo
soccer uniform

los pants
(ᶜel chándal)
jogging suit

las mallas
leggings

vocabulario • vocabulary

la fibra natural
natural fiber

sintético
synthetic

¿Se puede lavar a máquina?
Is it machine washable?

¿Le quedará a un niño de dos años? (ᶜ¿Le valdrá esto a un niño de dos años?)
Will this fit a two-year-old?

la ropa de caballero • men's clothing

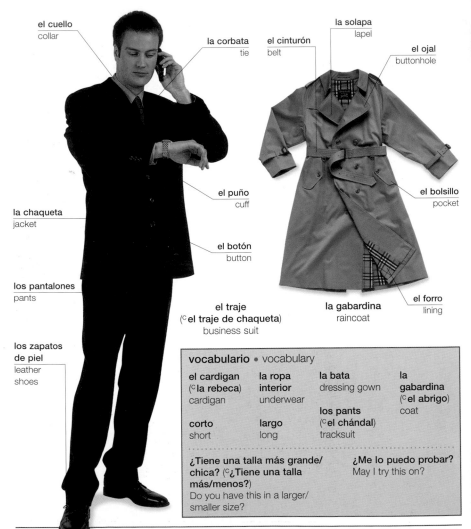

el cuello
collar

la corbata
tie

el cinturón
belt

la solapa
lapel

el ojal
buttonhole

el puño
cuff

la chaqueta
jacket

el bolsillo
pocket

el botón
button

los pantalones
pants

el traje
(ᶜ el traje de chaqueta)
business suit

la gabardina
raincoat

el forro
lining

los zapatos
de piel
leather
shoes

vocabulario • vocabulary

el cardigan (ᶜ **la rebeca**) cardigan	**la ropa interior** underwear	**la bata** dressing gown	**la gabardina** (ᶜ **el abrigo**) coat
		los pants (ᶜ **el chándal**) tracksuit	
corto short	**largo** long		

¿Tiene una talla más grande/ chica? (ᶜ**¿Tiene una talla más/menos?**)
Do you have this in a larger/ smaller size?

¿Me lo puedo probar?
May I try this on?

el saco (ᶜla chaqueta)
blazer

el saco sport
(ᶜla americana sport)
sport coat

el chaleco
vest

el cuello en V
(ᶜel cuello de pico)
V-neck

el cuello
redondo
crew neck

la camiseta
T-shirt

el chaquetón
parka

la sudadera
sweatshirt

la camisa
shirt

los tejanos
jeans

el suéter (ᶜel jersey)
sweater

la piyama (ᶜel pijama)
pajamas

la camiseta de tirantes
undershirt

la ropa casual
casual wear

los shorts (ᶜlos pantalones
cortos) | shorts

los calzoncillos
briefs

los boxers (ᶜlos calzoncillos
de pata) | boxer shorts

los calcetines
socks

la ropa de dama (ᶜ de señora) • women's clothing

el saco
(ᶜ la chaqueta)
jacket

la costura
seam

la manga
sleeve

largo
ankle length

el dobladillo
hem

la falda
skirt

hasta la rodilla
knee-length

los zapatos
shoes

formal
formal

sin
tirantes
strapless

sin mangas
sleeveless

el traje de noche
evening dress

el vestido
dress

la blusa
blouse

los pantalones
pants

casual (ᶜ sport)
casual

la lencería • lingerie

el tirante
strap

la bata
robe

el fondo
(ᶜ **la combinación**)
slip

la camisola
camisole

las ligas
garter belt

**el corsé con
liguero**
bustier

la media
stocking

las pantimedias
(ᶜ **las medias**)
panty hose

el brassiere
(ᶜ **el sujetador**)
bra

las pantaletas
(ᶜ **las bragas**)
panties

el camisón
nightgown

la boda • wedding

el
encaje
lace

el velo
veil

el ramo de flores
bouquet

la cola
train

el vestido de novia
wedding dress

vocabulario • vocabulary

el corsé corset	**la liga** garter
el brassiere (ᶜ **sujetador**) **deportivo** sports bra	**entallado** (ᶜ **sastre**) tailored
la hombrera shoulder pad	**con varillas** (ᶜ **con aros**) underwire
la cinturilla waistband	**al cuello y con los** **hombros al aire** halter neck

los accesorios • accessories

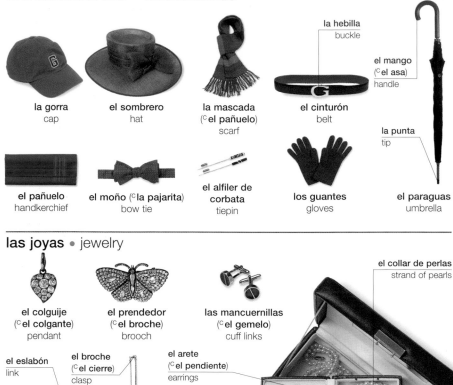

la gorra
cap

el sombrero
hat

la mascada
(^{C} **el pañuelo**)
scarf

la hebilla
buckle

el cinturón
belt

el mango
(^{C} el asa)
handle

la punta
tip

el pañuelo
handkerchief

el moño (^{C} **la pajarita**)
bow tie

el alfiler de corbata
tiepin

los guantes
gloves

el paraguas
umbrella

las joyas • jewelry

el colguije
(^{C} **el colgante**)
pendant

el prendedor
(^{C} **el broche**)
brooch

las mancuernillas
(^{C} **el gemelo**)
cuff links

el collar de perlas
strand of pearls

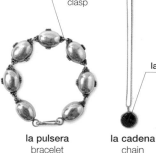

el eslabón
link

el broche
(^{C} el cierre)
clasp

el arete
(^{C} el pendiente)
earrings

el anillo
ring

la piedra
stone

el collar
necklace

la pulsera
bracelet

la cadena
chain

el reloj
watch

el joyero | jewelry box

las bolsas • bags

la cartera
wallet

el monedero
change purse

la bolsa (ᶜ **el bolso**)
shoulder bag

el cierre
clasp

la correa
shoulder strap

las asas
handles

la bolsa de viaje
duffel bag

el maletín
briefcase

la bolsa (ᶜ **el bolso**) **de mano**
handbag

la mochila
backpack

los zapatos • shoes

la agujeta
(ᶜ **el cordón**)
lace

la lengüeta
tongue

el ojal
eyelet

el tacón
heel

la suela
sole

el zapato de agujetas (ᶜ **de cordoneras**)
lace-up

la bota de trekking
hiking boot

el tenis (ᶜ **la zapatilla deportiva**)
sneaker

la bota
boot

la chancla
flip-flop

el zapato de caballero
dress shoe

el zapato de tacón
high-heeled shoe

la cuña
wedge

la sandalia
sandal

el mocasín
slip-on

la bailarina
pump

el cabello • hair

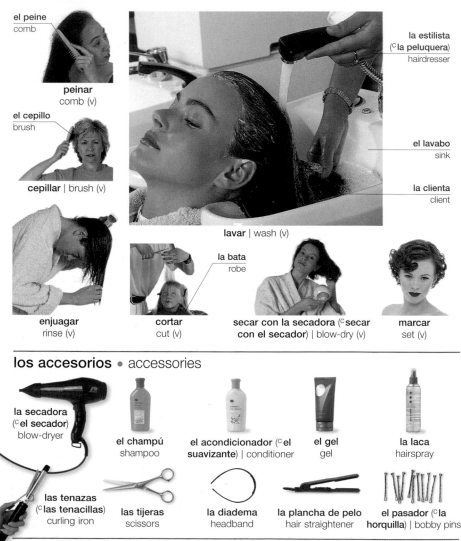

el peine
comb

peinar
comb (v)

el cepillo
brush

cepillar | brush (v)

la estilista
(ᶜ**la peluquera**)
hairdresser

el lavabo
sink

la clienta
client

lavar | wash (v)

enjuagar
rinse (v)

la bata
robe

cortar
cut (v)

secar con la secadora (ᶜ**secar con el secador**) | blow-dry (v)

marcar
set (v)

los accesorios • accessories

la secadora
(ᶜ**el secador**)
blow-dryer

el champú
shampoo

el acondicionador (ᶜ**el suavizante**) | conditioner

el gel
gel

la laca
hairspray

las tenazas
(ᶜ**las tenacillas**)
curling iron

las tijeras
scissors

la diadema
headband

la plancha de pelo
hair straightener

el pasador (ᶜ**la horquilla**) | bobby pins

los estilos • styles

la cola de caballo
ponytail

la trenza
braid

el chongo (ᶜel moño) francés
French twist

el chongo (ᶜel moño)
bun

las coletas
pigtails

el príncipe valiente (ᶜla melena) | bob

el pelo corto
crop

rizado
curly

la permanente
perm

lacio
straight

las raíces
roots

las luces (ᶜlos reflejos)
highlights

calvo
bald

la peluca
wig

vocabulario • vocabulary

la goma del pelo hair band	**graso** greasy
despuntar (ᶜcortar las puntas) trim (v)	**seco** dry
el peluquero (ᶜel barbero) barber	**alaciar (ᶜalisar)** straighten (v)
la caspa dandruff	**normal** normal
la orzuela (ᶜlas puntas abiertas) split ends	**el cuero cabelludo** scalp

los colores • colors

güero (ᶜrubio)
blonde

castaño
brunette

rojizo
auburn

pelirrojo
red

negro
black

gris
gray

blanco
white

teñido
dyed

la belleza • beauty

el tinte para el pelo
hair dye

la sombra
de ojos
eye shadow

el rímel
mascara

el delineador
(C el lápiz de ojos)
eyeliner

el rubor
(C el colorete)
blush

la base
(C el maquillaje de fondo)
foundation

el lápiz labial (C el pinta labios)
lipstick

el maquillaje • makeup

el lápiz de cejas
eyebrow pencil

el cepillo para las cejas
eyebrow brush

las pinzas
tweezers

el brillo de labios
lip gloss

el pincel de labios
lip brush

el lápiz de labios
lip liner

la brocha
brush

el lápiz corrector
concealer

el espejo
mirror

el maquillaje (C los
polvos compactos)
face powder

la borla
powder puff

la polvera | compact

los tratamientos de belleza •
beauty treatments

la mascarilla
face mask

la cama de rayos
ultravioletas
sunbed

la limpieza de cutis
facial

exfoliar
exfoliate (v)

la depilación a la cera
wax

la pedicura
pedicure

la manicura • manicure

el quitaesmalte
nail polish remover

la lima de uñas
nail file

el esmalte de uñas
nail polish

las tijeras de
uñas
nail scissors

el cortaúñas
nail clippers

los artículos de tocador •
toiletries

la crema
limpiadora
cleanser

el tónico
toner

la crema
hidratante
moisturizer

la crema
bronceadora
(^Cautobronceadora)
self-tanning lotion

el perfume
perfume

el agua de
colonia
eau de toilette

vocabulario • vocabulary

el cutis complexion	**graso** oily	**el bronceado** tan
claro fair	**sensible** sensitive	**el tatuaje** tattoo
moreno dark	**hipoalergénico** hypoallergenic	**antiarrugas** antiwrinkle
seco dry	**el tono** shade	**las bolas de algodón** cotton balls

la salud
health

la enfermedad • illness

el dolor de
cabeza
headache

la hemorragia
nasal
nosebleed

la tos
cough

la fiebre | fever

el estornudo
sneeze

el resfriado
cold

la gripe
flu

el inhalador
inhaler

el asma
asthma

los calambres
cramps

la náusea
nausea

la varicela
chicken pox

el sarpullido
rash

---

vocabulario • vocabulary

la aplopejía (^Cel derrame cerebral) stroke	la fiebre del heno hay fever	la infección infection	el dolor de estómago stomachache	la migraña (^Cla jaqueca) migraine	la diarrea diarrhea
la diabetes diabetes	la alergia allergy	el eccema eczema	el resfriado chill	vomitar vomit (v)	el sarampión measles
el ataque cardiaco (^Cel infarto de miocardio) heart attack	la presión arterial (^Cla tensión arterial) blood pressure	el virus virus	desmayarse faint (v)	la epilepsia epilepsy	las paperas mumps

el doctor (ᶜ el médico) • doctor
la consulta • consultation

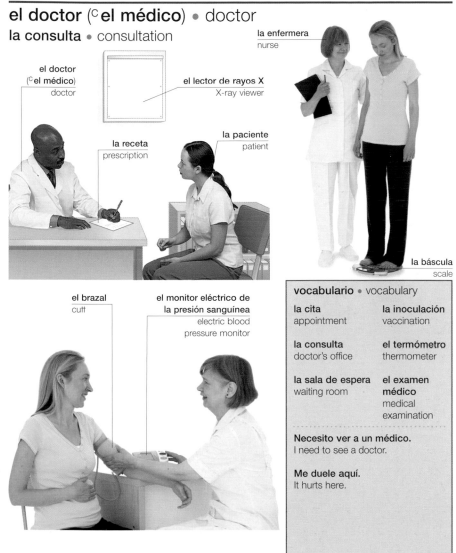

la enfermera
nurse

el doctor
(ᶜ el médico)
doctor

el lector de rayos X
X-ray viewer

la receta
prescription

la paciente
patient

la báscula
scale

el brazal
cuff

el monitor eléctrico de
la presión sanguínea
electric blood
pressure monitor

vocabulario • vocabulary

la cita
appointment

la inoculación
vaccination

la consulta
doctor's office

el termómetro
thermometer

la sala de espera
waiting room

el examen
médico
medical
examination

Necesito ver a un médico.
I need to see a doctor.

Me duele aquí.
It hurts here.

la lesión • injury

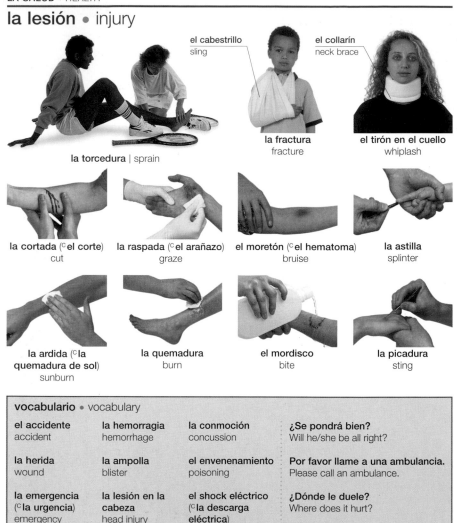

el cabestrillo
sling

el collarín
neck brace

la fractura
fracture

el tirón en el cuello
whiplash

la torcedura | sprain

la cortada (^C**el corte**)
cut

la raspada (^C**el arañazo**)
graze

el moretón (^C**el hematoma**)
bruise

la astilla
splinter

la ardida (^C**la quemadura de sol**)
sunburn

la quemadura
burn

el mordisco
bite

la picadura
sting

---

vocabulario • vocabulary

el accidente accident	**la hemorragia** hemorrhage	**la conmoción** concussion	**¿Se pondrá bien?** Will he/she be all right?
la herida wound	**la ampolla** blister	**el envenenamiento** poisoning	**Por favor llame a una ambulancia.** Please call an ambulance.
la emergencia (^C**la urgencia**) emergency	**la lesión en la cabeza** head injury	**el shock eléctrico** (^C**la descarga eléctrica**) electric shock	**¿Dónde le duele?** Where does it hurt?

los primeros auxilios • first aid

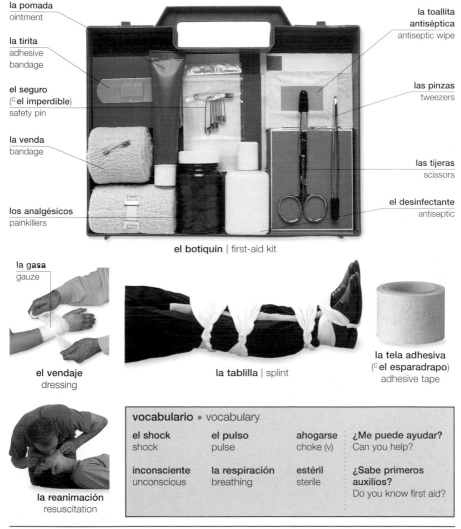

la pomada
ointment

la tirita
adhesive
bandage

el seguro
(ᶜ **el imperdible**)
safety pin

la venda
bandage

los analgésicos
painkillers

**la toallita
antiséptica**
antiseptic wipe

las pinzas
tweezers

las tijeras
scissors

el desinfectante
antiseptic

el botiquín | first-aid kit

la gasa
gauze

el vendaje
dressing

la tablilla | splint

la tela adhesiva
(ᶜ **el esparadrapo**)
adhesive tape

la reanimación
resuscitation

vocabulario • vocabulary			
el shock shock	**el pulso** pulse	**ahogarse** choke (v)	**¿Me puede ayudar?** Can you help?
inconsciente unconscious	**la respiración** breathing	**estéril** sterile	**¿Sabe primeros auxilios?** Do you know first aid?

el hospital • hospital

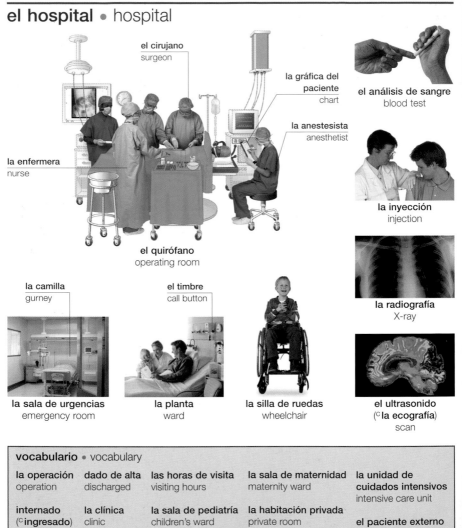

el cirujano
surgeon

la gráfica del
paciente
chart

la anestesista
anesthetist

la enfermera
nurse

el quirófano
operating room

el análisis de sangre
blood test

la inyección
injection

la radiografía
X-ray

la camilla
gurney

el timbre
call button

la sala de urgencias
emergency room

la planta
ward

la silla de ruedas
wheelchair

el ultrasonido
(ᶜ la ecografía)
scan

---

vocabulario • vocabulary

la operación operation	**dado de alta** discharged	**las horas de visita** visiting hours	**la sala de maternidad** maternity ward	**la unidad de** **cuidados intensivos** intensive care unit
internado (ᶜ **ingresado**) admitted	**la clínica** clinic	**la sala de pediatría** children's ward	**la habitación privada** private room	**el paciente externo** outpatient

---

los servicios • departments

la otorrinolaringología
ENT

la cardiología
cardiology

la ortopedia
orthopedics

la ginecología
gynecology

la fisioterapia
physiotherapy

la dermatología
dermatology

la pediatría
pediatrics

la radiología
radiology

la cirugía
surgery

la maternidad
maternity

la psiquiatría
psychiatry

la oftalmología
ophthalmology

---

vocabulario • vocabulary

la neurología neurology	**la urología** urology	**la cirugía plástica** plastic surgery	**la patología** pathology	**el resultado** result
la oncología oncology	**la endocrinología** endocrinology	**la referencia** (ᶜ **el volante**) referral	**el análisis** test	**el especialista** specialist

---

el dentista • dentist

el diente • tooth

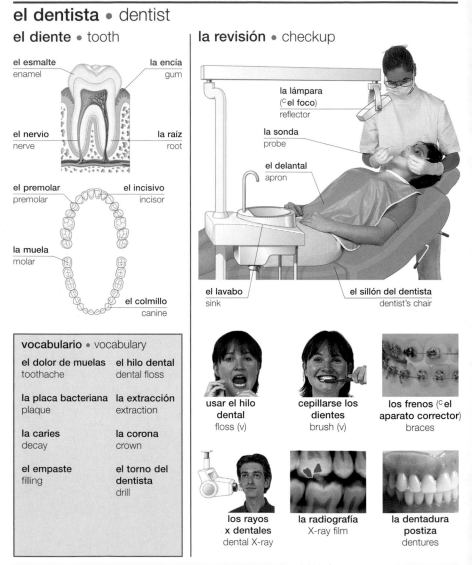

el esmalte
enamel

la encía
gum

el nervio
nerve

la raíz
root

el premolar
premolar

el incisivo
incisor

la muela
molar

el colmillo
canine

la revisión • checkup

la lámpara
(^Cel foco)
reflector

la sonda
probe

el delantal
apron

el lavabo
sink

el sillón del dentista
dentist's chair

vocabulario • vocabulary

el dolor de muelas toothache	el hilo dental dental floss
la placa bacteriana plaque	la extracción extraction
la caries decay	la corona crown
el empaste filling	el torno del dentista drill

usar el hilo dental
floss (v)

cepillarse los dientes
brush (v)

los frenos (^Cel aparato corrector)
braces

los rayos x dentales
dental X-ray

la radiografía
X-ray film

la dentadura postiza
dentures

el óptico • optometrist

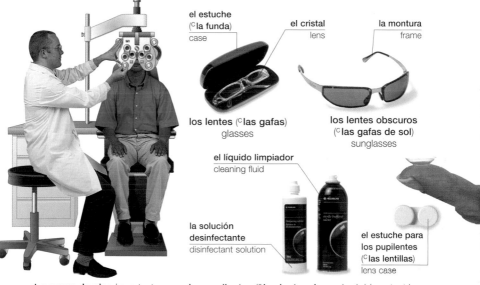

el estuche
(^C la funda)
case

el cristal
lens

la montura
frame

los lentes (^C las gafas)
glasses

los lentes obscuros
(^C las gafas de sol)
sunglasses

el líquido limpiador
cleaning fluid

la solución
desinfectante
disinfectant solution

el estuche para
los pupilentes
(^C las lentillas)
lens case

el examen de ojos | eye test

los pupilentes (^C las lentes de contacto) | contact lenses

el ojo • eye

la ceja
eyebrow

el párpado
eyelid

la pupila
pupil

la pestaña
eyelash

el iris
iris

la retina
retina

el cristalino
lens

el nervio óptico
optic nerve

la córnea
cornea

vocabulario • vocabulary	
la vista vision	el astigmatismo astigmatism
la dioptría diopter	la hipermetropía farsighted
la lágrima tear	la miopía nearsighted
la catarata cataract	bifocal bifocal

el embarazo • pregnancy

la prueba del embarazo
pregnancy test

el ultrasonido (ᶜla ecografía)
scan

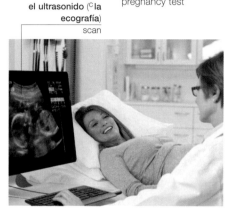

el ultrasonido | ultrasound

la placenta
placenta

el cordón umbilical
umbilical cord

el cuello uterino
cervix

el útero
uterus

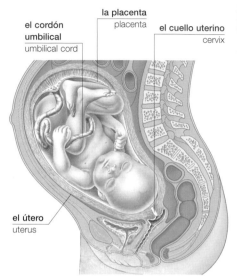

el feto | fetus

---

vocabulario • vocabulary

la ovulación ovulation	**prenatal** prenatal	**la contracción** contraction	**la dilatación** dilation	**el parto** delivery	**prematuro** premature
la concepción conception	**el trimestre** trimestre	**romper aguas** break water (v)	**la epidural** epidural	**el nacimiento** birth	**el ginecólogo** gynecologist
embarazada (ᶜ**encinta**) expecting	**el embrión** embryo	**el líquido amniótico** amniotic fluid	**la cesárea** cesarean section	**el aborto espontáneo** miscarriage	**el obstetra** (ᶜ**el tocólogo**) obstetrician
embarazada pregnant	**la matriz** womb	**la amniocentesis** amniocentesis	**la episiotomía** episiotomy	**las puntadas** (ᶜ**los puntos**) stitches	**de espaldas** (ᶜ**el parto de nalgas**) breech birth

---

el parto • childbirth

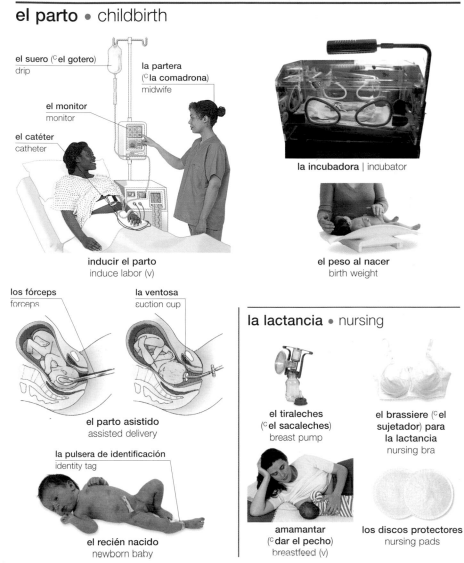

el suero (^Cel gotero)
drip

la partera
(^Cla comadrona)
midwife

el monitor
monitor

el catéter
catheter

inducir el parto
induce labor (v)

la incubadora | incubator

el peso al nacer
birth weight

los fórceps
forceps

la ventosa
suction cup

el parto asistido
assisted delivery

la pulsera de identificación
identity tag

el recién nacido
newborn baby

la lactancia • nursing

el tiraleches
(^Cel sacaleches)
breast pump

el brassiere (^Cel
sujetador) para
la lactancia
nursing bra

amamantar
(^Cdar el pecho)
breastfeed (v)

los discos protectores
nursing pads

las terapias alternativas • alternative therapy

la postura de yoga
yoga pose

la colchoneta
mat

el yoga | yoga

el masaje
massage

el shiatsu
shiatsu

la quiropráctica
chiropractic

la osteopatía
osteopathy

la reflexología
reflexology

la meditación
meditation

el terapeuta
counselor

la terapia de grupo
group therapy

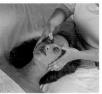

el reiki
reiki

la acupuntura
acupuncture

la ayurveda
ayurveda

la hipnoterapia
hypnotherapy

los aceites esenciales
essential oils

el herbolario
herbalism

la aromaterapia
aromatherapy

la homeopatía
homeopathy

la acupresión
acupressure

la terapeuta
therapist

la psicoterapia
psychotherapy

vocabulario • vocabulary

la cristaloterapia crystal healing	**la naturopatía** naturopathy	**la relajación** relaxation	**la hierba** herb
la hidroterapia hydrotherapy	**el feng shui** feng shui	**el estrés** stress	**el suplemento** supplement

la casa
home

la casa • house

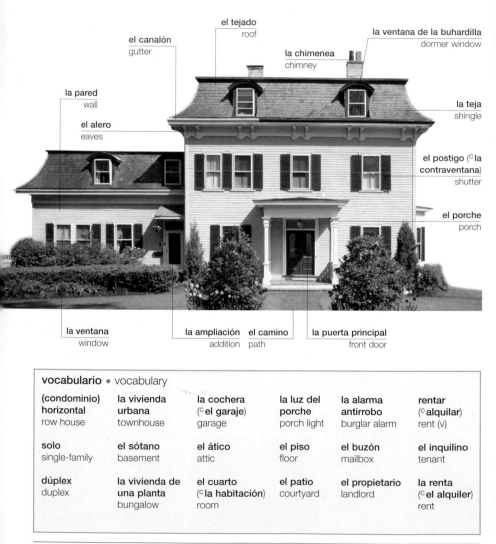

el tejado
roof

la ventana de la buhardilla
dormer window

la chimenea
chimney

el canalón
gutter

la pared
wall

el alero
eaves

la teja
shingle

el postigo (^Cla contraventana)
shutter

el porche
porch

la ventana
window

la ampliación
addition

el camino
path

la puerta principal
front door

vocabulario • vocabulary

(condominio) horizontal row house	**la vivienda urbana** townhouse	**la cochera** (^C**el garaje**) garage	**la luz del porche** porch light	**la alarma antirrobo** burglar alarm	**rentar** (^C**alquilar**) rent (v)
solo single-family	**el sótano** basement	**el ático** attic	**el piso** floor	**el buzón** mailbox	**el inquilino** tenant
dúplex duplex	**la vivienda de una planta** bungalow	**el cuarto** (^C**la habitación**) room	**el patio** courtyard	**el propietario** landlord	**la renta** (^C**el alquiler**) rent

la entrada • entrance

el pasamanos
hand rail

la escalera
staircase

el descanso
(C el descansillo)
landing

el barandal
(C la barandilla)
banister

el vestíbulo
foyer

el timbre
doorbell

el tapete (C el felpudo)
doormat

la aldaba
door knocker

la llave
key

la cadena
door chain

la cerradura
lock

el cerrojo
bolt

el departamento
(C el piso) •
apartment

el balcón
balcony

el edificio
apartment building

el interfono
intercom

el elevador (C el ascensor)
elevator

las instalaciones internas • internal systems

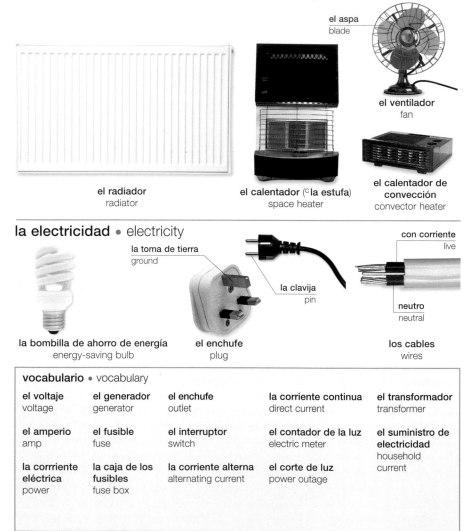

el aspa
blade

el ventilador
fan

el radiador
radiator

el calentador (^C **la estufa**)
space heater

el calentador de convección
convector heater

la electricidad • electricity

la toma de tierra
ground

con corriente
live

la clavija
pin

neutro
neutral

la bombilla de ahorro de energía
energy-saving bulb

el enchufe
plug

los cables
wires

---

vocabulario • vocabulary

el voltaje voltage	**el generador** generator	**el enchufe** outlet	**la corriente continua** direct current	**el transformador** transformer
el amperio amp	**el fusible** fuse	**el interruptor** switch	**el contador de la luz** electric meter	**el suministro de electricidad** household current
la corriente eléctrica power	**la caja de los fusibles** fuse box	**la corriente alterna** alternating current	**el corte de luz** power outage	

la fontanería • plumbing

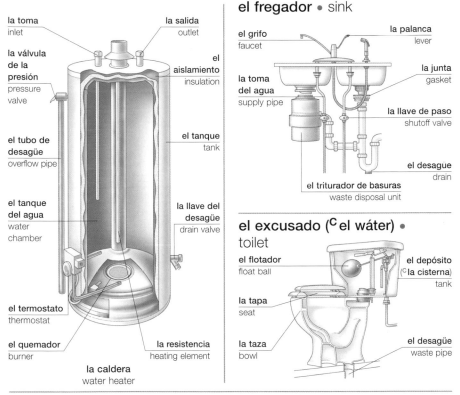

la toma
inlet

la salida
outlet

la válvula
de la
presión
pressure
valve

el
aislamiento
insulation

el tubo de
desagüe
overflow pipe

el tanque
tank

el tanque
del agua
water
chamber

la llave del
desagüe
drain valve

el termostato
thermostat

el quemador
burner

la resistencia
heating element

la caldera
water heater

el fregador • sink

el grifo
faucet

la palanca
lever

la toma
del agua
supply pipe

la junta
gasket

la llave de paso
shutoff valve

el desague
drain

el triturador de basuras
waste disposal unit

el excusado (^Cel wáter) • toilet

el flotador
float ball

el depósito
(^Cla cisterna)
tank

la tapa
seat

la taza
bowl

el desagüe
waste pipe

la eliminación de desechos • waste disposal

la botella
bottle

la tapa
lid

el pedal
pedal

**el cubo para
reciclar**
recycling bin

el cubo de la basura
trash can

**el armario para
clasificar la basura**
sorting unit

**los desperdicios
orgánicos**
organic waste

la sala (^Cel cuarto de estar) • living room

el arbotante
(^Cel aplique)
wall light

la chimenea
fireplace

el techo
ceiling

la lámpara
lamp

el jarrón
vase

el cojín
pillow

la mesa de
centro (^Cla
mesa de
café)
coffee table

el sofá
sofa

el piso
(^Cel suelo)
floor

español • english

el marco
frame

el cuadro
painting

la cortina
curtain

el visillo
sheer curtain

la persiana (^Cel estor
de láminas)
Venetian blind

el estor
roller shade

la moldura
molding

el sillón
armchair

el librero
(^Cla estantería)
bookshelf

el sofá-cama
sofa bed

el tapete
(^Cla alfombra)
rug

el estudio (^Cel despacho) | study

el comedor • dining room

la pimienta
pepper

la sal
salt

la mesa
table

la vajilla
crockery

la silla
chair

el respaldo
back

el asiento
seat

los cubiertos
cutlery

la pata
leg

vocabulario • vocabulary

servir serve (v)	**la comida** meal	**el desayuno** breakfast	**hambriento** hungry	**el anfitrión** host	**Estaba riquísimo.** (ᶜ**Estaba buenísimo.**) That was delicious.
comer eat (v)	**el mantel** tablecloth	**la comida** lunch	**lleno** full	**la anfitriona** hostess	**Estoy lleno, gracias.** I've had enough, thank you.
poner la mesa set the table (v)	**el mantel individual** place mat	**la cena** dinner	**la ración** portion	**el invitado** guest	**¿Puedo comer otro poco?** (ᶜ**¿Puedo repetir, por favor?**) Can I have some more, please?

la vajilla y los cubiertos • crockery and cutlery

la cucharilla de café
teaspoon

la taza
mug

la taza de café
coffee cup

la taza de té
teacup

el plato
plate

el plato sopero
(ᶜ **el bol**)
bowl

la copa de vino
wine glass

el vaso
tumbler

la cafetera de émbolo
French press

la tetera
teapot

la jarra
pitcher

la taza para el huevo
(ᶜ **la huevera**)
egg cup

la cristalería
glassware

el servilletero
napkin ring

el plato del pan
side plate

el plato
(ᶜ **el plato llano**)
dinner plate

el plato sopero
soup bowl

la cuchara sopera
soup spoon

la servilleta
napkin

el tenedor
fork

el lugar en la mesa
place setting

la cuchara
spoon

el cuchillo
knife

la cocina • kitchen

los estantes
shelves

el frente de la cocina
backsplash

el grifo
faucet

el fregadero
sink

el cajón
drawer

el extractor
ventilation hood

la placa vitro-cerámica
ceramic stovetop

la plancha
(^{C}la encimera)
countertop

el horno
oven

la gaveta
(^{C}el armario)
cabinet

los electrodomésticos • appliances

el microondas
microwave oven

el recipiente (^{C}el cuenco mezclador)
mixing bowl

la tapa
lid

la cuchilla
blade

la jarra para hervir
(^{C}el hervidor)
electric kettle

el tostador
toaster

el multimezclador
(^{C}el robot de cocina)
food processor

la licuadora
blender

la lavavajilla
(^{C}el friegaplatos)
dishwasher

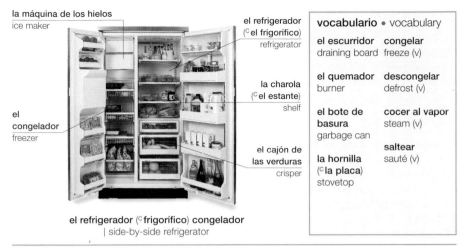

la máquina de los hielos
ice maker

el refrigerador
(ᶜel frigorífico)
refrigerator

la charola
(ᶜel estante)
shelf

el congelador
freezer

el cajón de
las verduras
crisper

el refrigerador (ᶜfrigorífico) congelador
| side-by-side refrigerator

vocabulario • vocabulary	
el escurridor draining board	**congelar** freeze (v)
el quemador burner	**descongelar** defrost (v)
el bote de basura garbage can	**cocer al vapor** steam (v)
la hornilla (ᶜla placa) stovetop	**saltear** sauté (v)

cocinar • cooking

pelar
peel (v)

cortar
slice (v)

rallar
grate (v)

vaciar (ᶜechar)
pour (v)

mezclar
mix (v)

batir
whisk (v)

hervir
boil (v)

freír
fry (v)

amasar (ᶜextender)
con el rodillo | roll (v)

remover
stir (v)

**cocer a fuego
lento**
simmer (v)

escalfar
poach (v)

hornear
(ᶜcocer al horno)
bake (v)

asar
roast (v)

asar a la parrilla
broil (v)

los utensilios de cocina • kitchenware

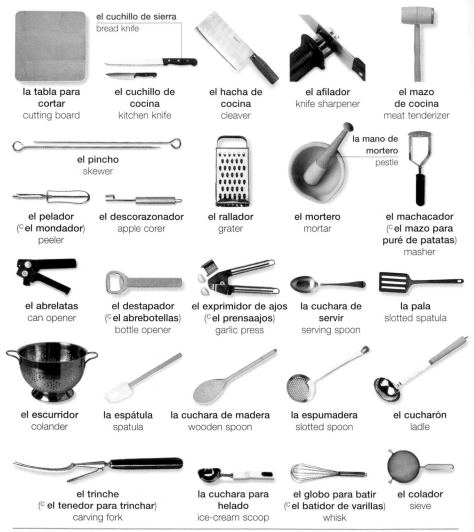

la tabla para cortar
cutting board

el cuchillo de sierra
bread knife

el cuchillo de cocina
kitchen knife

el hacha de cocina
cleaver

el afilador
knife sharpener

el mazo de cocina
meat tenderizer

el pincho
skewer

la mano de mortero
pestle

el pelador
(ᶜ **el mondador**)
peeler

el descorazonador
apple corer

el rallador
grater

el mortero
mortar

el machacador
(ᶜ **el mazo para puré de patatas**)
masher

el abrelatas
can opener

el destapador
(ᶜ **el abrebotellas**)
bottle opener

el exprimidor de ajos
(ᶜ **el prensaajos**)
garlic press

la cuchara de servir
serving spoon

la pala
slotted spatula

el escurridor
colander

la espátula
spatula

la cuchara de madera
wooden spoon

la espumadera
slotted spoon

el cucharón
ladle

el trinche
(ᶜ **el tenedor para trinchar**)
carving fork

la cuchara para helado
ice-cream scoop

el globo para batir
(ᶜ **el batidor de varillas**)
whisk

el colador
sieve

la tapa
lid

antiadherente
nonstick

la sartén
frying pan

la cacerola
(ᶜ **el cazo**)
saucepan

la parrilla
grill pan

el wok
wok

la olla (ᶜ **la
cazuela**) **de barro**
earthenware dish

de cristal
glass

resistente al horno
ovenproof

la ensaladera
(ᶜ **el cuenco**)
mixing bowl

el molde para suflé
soufflé dish

**la fuente para
gratinar**
gratin dish

**el molde
individual**
ramekin

la cazuela
casserole dish

la repostería • baking cakes

**la báscula de
cocina**
scale

la taza medidora
(ᶜ **la jarra graduada**)
measuring cup

**el molde para
pastel** (ᶜ **bizcocho**)
cake pan

el molde redondo
pie pan

la flanera
quiche pan

la brocha de cocina
pastry brush

el rodillo de cocina
rolling pin

la dulla (ᶜ **la manga pastelera**)
piping bag

**el molde para
panqués**
(ᶜ **magdalenas**)
muffin pan

la charola (ᶜ **la
bandeja**) **de horno**
cookie sheet

la rejilla
cooling rack

el guante (ᶜ **la
manopla**) **de cocina**
oven mitt

el delantal
apron

la recámara (^C el dormitorio) • bedroom

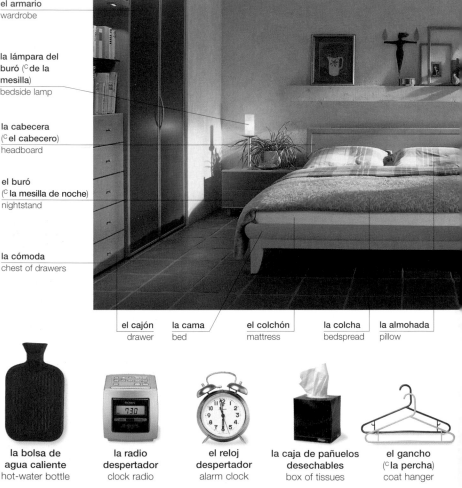

el armario
wardrobe

la lámpara del
buró (^C de la
mesilla)
bedside lamp

la cabecera
(^C el cabecero)
headboard

el buró
(^C la mesilla de noche)
nightstand

la cómoda
chest of drawers

el cajón	la cama	el colchón	la colcha	la almohada
drawer	bed	mattress	bedspread	pillow

**la bolsa de
agua caliente**
hot-water bottle

**la radio
despertador**
clock radio

**el reloj
despertador**
alarm clock

**la caja de pañuelos
desechables**
box of tissues

el gancho
(^C la percha)
coat hanger

la ropa de cama • bed linen

el espejo
mirror

el tocador
dressing
table

el suelo
floor

**la funda de la
almohada**
pillowcase

la sábana
sheet

el cubrecanapé
dust ruffle

el edredón
comforter

la colcha
quilt

la cobija
(ᶜ **la manta**)
blanket

vocabulario • vocabulary

la cama individual twin bed	**el pie de la cama** footboard	**el insomnio** insomnia	**despertarse** wake up (v)	**roncar** snore (v)
la cama matrimonial (ᶜ **de matrimonio**) full bed	**el resorte** (ᶜ **el somier**) bedspring	**acostarse** go to bed (v)	**levantarse** get up (v)	**poner el despertador** set the alarm (v)
la cobija (ᶜ **la manta**) **eléctrica** electric blanket	**el tapete** (ᶜ **la moqueta**) carpet	**dormirse** go to sleep (v)	**hacer la cama** make the bed (v)	**el armario empotrado** closet

el cuarto de baño • bathroom

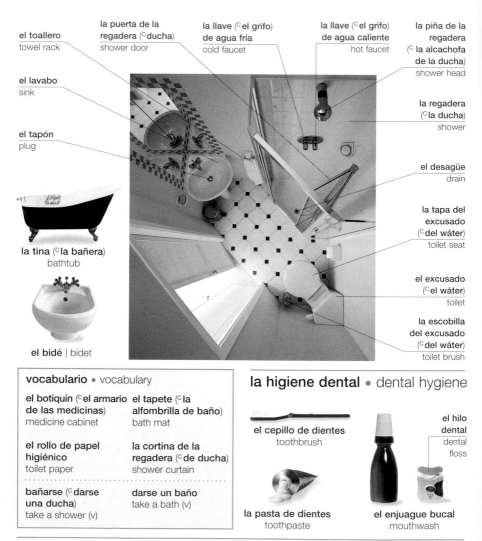

el toallero
towel rack

la puerta de la regadera (ᶜ**ducha**)
shower door

la llave (ᶜ**el grifo**) **de agua fría**
cold faucet

la llave (ᶜ**el grifo**) **de agua caliente**
hot faucet

la piña de la regadera (ᶜ **la alcachofa de la ducha**)
shower head

el lavabo
sink

la regadera (ᶜ**la ducha**)
shower

el tapón
plug

el desagüe
drain

la tina (ᶜ**la bañera**)
bathtub

la tapa del excusado (ᶜ**del wáter**)
toilet seat

el excusado (ᶜ**el wáter**)
toilet

la escobilla del excusado (ᶜ**del wáter**)
toilet brush

el bidé | bidet

vocabulario • vocabulary

el botiquín (ᶜ**el armario de las medicinas**)
medicine cabinet

el tapete (ᶜ**la alfombrilla de baño**)
bath mat

el rollo de papel higiénico
toilet paper

la cortina de la regadera (ᶜ**de ducha**)
shower curtain

bañarse (ᶜ**darse una ducha**)
take a shower (v)

darse un baño
take a bath (v)

la higiene dental • dental hygiene

el cepillo de dientes
toothbrush

el hilo dental
dental floss

la pasta de dientes
toothpaste

el enjuague bucal
mouthwash

la esponja
sponge

la piedra pómez
pumice stone

el cepillo para la
espalda
back brush

el desodorante
deodorant

la jabonera
soap dish

el shampoo para el cuerpo
(C el gel de ducha)
shower gel

el jabón
soap

la crema para la cara
face cream

el gel de baño
bubble bath

la toalla de mano
(C de lavabo)
hand towel

la toalla de
baño
bath towel

las toallas
towels

la crema para el cuerpo
(C la leche del cuerpo)
body lotion

el talco (C los
polvos de talco)
talcum powder

la bata
(C el albornoz)
bathrobe

el afeitado • shaving

la rasuradora
(C la maquinilla
eléctrica)
electric razor

la espuma de afeitar
shaving foam

la navaja de afeitar desechable
(C la cuchilla de afeitar
desechable) | disposable razor

la hoja de
afeitar
razor blade

el aftershave
aftershave

la habitación de los niños • nursery

el cuidado del bebé • baby care

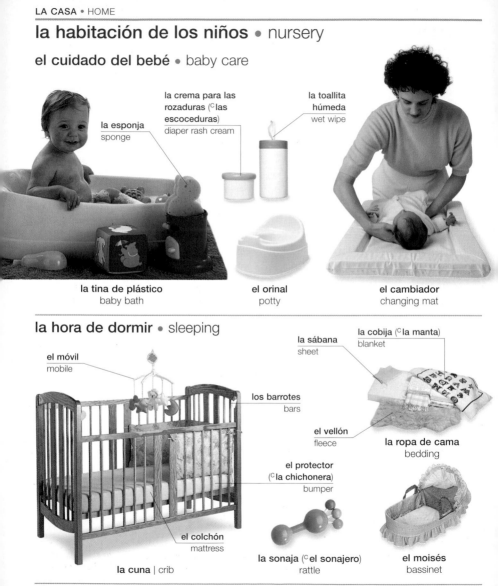

la crema para las rozaduras (ᶜ las escoceduras)
diaper rash cream

la esponja
sponge

la toallita húmeda
wet wipe

la tina de plástico
baby bath

el orinal
potty

el cambiador
changing mat

la hora de dormir • sleeping

el móvil
mobile

la sábana
sheet

la cobija (ᶜ la manta)
blanket

los barrotes
bars

el vellón
fleece

la ropa de cama
bedding

el protector (ᶜ la chichonera)
bumper

el colchón
mattress

la cuna | crib

la sonaja (ᶜ el sonajero)
rattle

el moisés
bassinet

los juegos • playing

la muñeca
doll

el muñeco de peluche
stuffed toy

la casa de muñecas
dollhouse

la casa de juguete
playhouse

el oso de peluche
teddy bear

el juguete
toy

la pelota
ball

el cesto de los juguetes
toy basket

el corral (ᶜel parque)
playpen

la seguridad • safety

el cierre de seguridad
child lock

el intercomunicador
(ᶜel escuchabebés)
baby monitor

la barrera de seguridad
stair gate

la comida • eating

la periquera (ᶜla trona)
high chair

el chupón
(ᶜla tetina)
nipple

la taza
drinking cup

la mamila (ᶜel biberón)
bottle

el paseo • going out

la capota
hood

la carriola
(ᶜla silleta de paseo)
stroller

la carriola
(ᶜel cochecito de niños)
baby carriage

el pañal
diaper

el bambineto (ᶜel capazo) | carrier

la pañalera (ᶜla bolsa del bebé) | diaper bag

la cangurera (ᶜla mochila de bebé) | baby sling

la lavandería (^C el lavadero) • utility room

la colada • laundry

la ropa limpia
clean clothes

la ropa sucia
dirty laundry

el cesto de la ropa sucia (^C **de la colada**)
laundry basket

la lavadora
washing machine

la lavadora secadora
washer-dryer

la secadora
tumble dryer

el tendedero (^C **la cuerda para tender la ropa**)
clothesline

la plancha
iron

la pinza para la ropa
clothespin

secar
dry (v)

el burro (^C **la tabla**) **de la plancha** | ironing board

---

vocabulario • vocabulary

cargar load (v)	**centrifugar** spin (v)	**planchar** iron (v)	**¿Cómo funciona la lavadora?** How do I operate the washing machine?
aclarar rinse (v)	**la centrífuga** (^C **la centrifugadora**) spin dryer	**el suavizante** fabric softener	**¿Cuál es el programa para la ropa de color/blanca?** What is the setting for colors/whites?

---

el equipo de limpieza • cleaning equipment

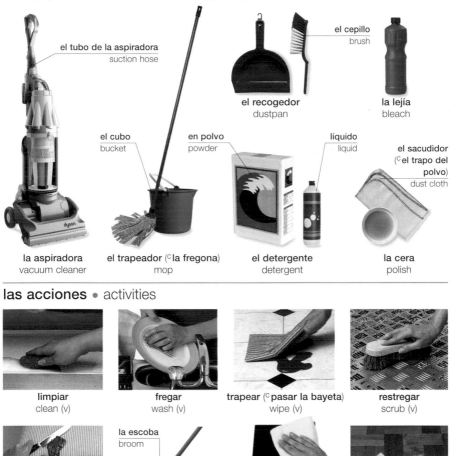

el tubo de la aspiradora
suction hose

el cepillo
brush

el recogedor
dustpan

la lejía
bleach

el cubo
bucket

en polvo
powder

líquido
liquid

el sacudidor
(ᶜel trapo del
polvo)
dust cloth

la aspiradora
vacuum cleaner

el trapeador (ᶜla fregona)
mop

el detergente
detergent

la cera
polish

las acciones • activities

limpiar
clean (v)

fregar
wash (v)

trapear (ᶜpasar la bayeta)
wipe (v)

restregar
scrub (v)

raspar
scrape (v)

la escoba
broom

barrer
sweep (v)

sacudir (ᶜlimpiar el polvo)
dust (v)

pulir (ᶜsacar brillo)
polish (v)

el taller • workshop

el cabezal
chuck

la broca
drill bit

la batería
battery pack

la sierra de vaivén
jigsaw

el taladro inalámbrico
cordless drill

el taladro eléctrico
electric drill

la pistola para encolar
glue gun

la abrazadera
clamp

la cuchilla
blade

el tornillo (ᶜ el torno)
de banco | vise

la lijadora
sander

la sierra circular
circular saw

el banco de trabajo
workbench

el pegamento (ᶜ la
cola) de carpintero
wood glue

el organizador de
las herramientas
tool rack

la rebajadora
router

el taladro manual
bit brace

las virutas de madera
wood shavings

la extensión
(ᶜ el alargador)
extension cord

las técnicas • techniques

cortar
cut (v)

serrar
saw (v)

taladrar
drill (v)

clavar
hammer (v)

cepillar (^Calisar)
plane (v)

tornear
turn (v)

la soldadura
(^Cel hilo de estaño)
solder

tallar
carve (v)

soldar
solder (v)

los materiales • materials

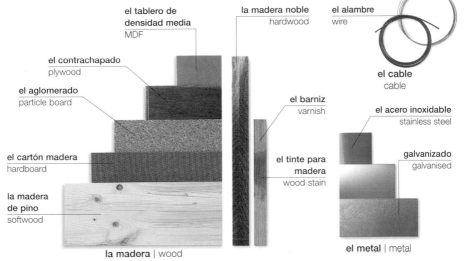

el tablero de
densidad media
MDF

la madera noble
hardwood

el alambre
wire

el contrachapado
plywood

el cable
cable

el aglomerado
particle board

el barniz
varnish

el acero inoxidable
stainless steel

el cartón madera
hardboard

el tinte para
madera
wood stain

galvanizado
galvanised

la madera
de pino
softwood

el metal | metal

la madera | wood

la caja de las herramientas • toolbox

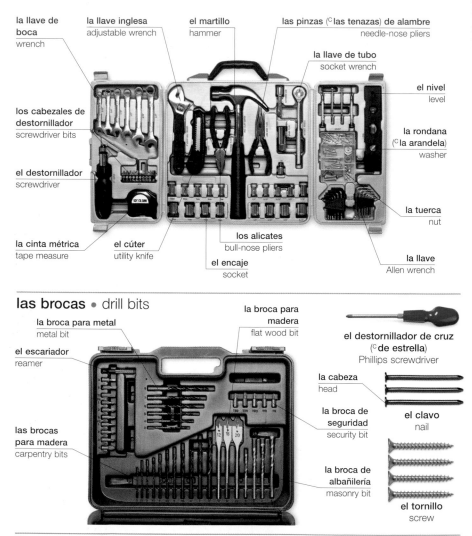

la llave de
boca
wrench

la llave inglesa
adjustable wrench

el martillo
hammer

las pinzas (^C las tenazas) de alambre
needle-nose pliers

la llave de tubo
socket wrench

el nivel
level

los cabezales de
destornillador
screwdriver bits

la rondana
(^C la arandela)
washer

el destornillador
screwdriver

la tuerca
nut

la cinta métrica
tape measure

el cúter
utility knife

los alicates
bull-nose pliers

el encaje
socket

la llave
Allen wrench

las brocas • drill bits

la broca para
madera
flat wood bit

la broca para metal
metal bit

el destornillador de cruz
(^C de estrella)
Phillips screwdriver

el escariador
reamer

la cabeza
head

la broca de
seguridad
security bit

el clavo
nail

las brocas
para madera
carpentry bits

la broca de
albañilería
masonry bit

el tornillo
screw

el pelacables
wire strippers

el cortaalambres
wire cutters

el soldador
soldering iron

la cinta aislante
electrical tape

la soldadura
solder

el escalpelo
craft knife

la sierra de calar
fretsaw

el serrucho de costilla | tenon saw

las gafas de seguridad
safety goggles

el cepillo
plane

el serrucho
handsaw

la caja para cortar en inglete
miter block

la sierra para metales
hacksaw

el taladro manual
hand drill

la lana de acero
steel wool

el papel de lija
sandpaper

las tenazas
wrench

el formón
chisel

el destapacaños
(ᶜel desatascador)
plunger

la lima
file

la piedra afiladora
whetstone

el cortatuberías | pipe cutter

la decoración • decorating

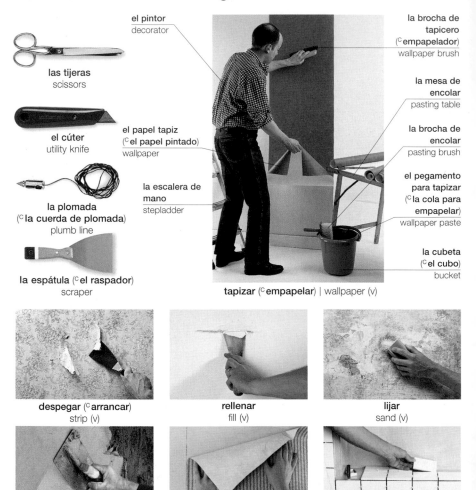

el pintor
decorator

las tijeras
scissors

el cúter
utility knife

el papel tapiz
(Cel papel pintado)
wallpaper

la plomada
(Cla cuerda de plomada)
plumb line

la escalera de mano
stepladder

la espátula (Cel raspador)
scraper

la brocha de tapicero
(Cempapelador)
wallpaper brush

la mesa de encolar
pasting table

la brocha de encolar
pasting brush

el pegamento para tapizar
(Cla cola para empapelar)
wallpaper paste

la cubeta
(Cel cubo)
bucket

tapizar (Cempapelar) | wallpaper (v)

despegar (Carrancar)
strip (v)

rellenar
fill (v)

lijar
sand (v)

enyesar | plaster (v)

empapelar | hang (v)

poner azulejos (Calicatar) | tile (v)

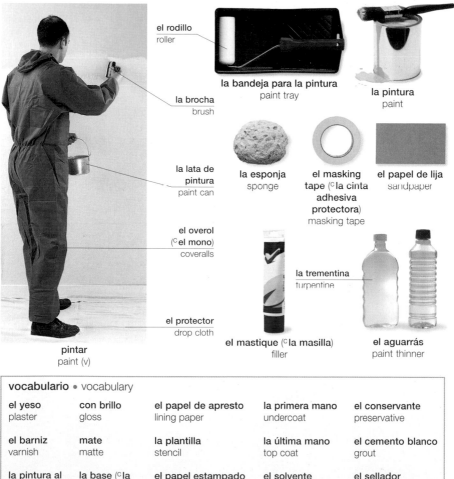

el rodillo
roller

la bandeja para la pintura
paint tray

la pintura
paint

la brocha
brush

la esponja
sponge

el masking tape (ᶜla cinta adhesiva protectora)
masking tape

el papel de lija
sandpaper

la lata de pintura
paint can

el overol (ᶜel mono)
coveralls

la trementina
turpentine

el protector
drop cloth

el mastique (ᶜla masilla)
filler

el aguarrás
paint thinner

pintar
paint (v)

---

vocabulario • vocabulary

el yeso plaster	con brillo gloss	el papel de apresto lining paper	la primera mano undercoat	el conservante preservative
el barniz varnish	mate matte	la plantilla stencil	la última mano top coat	el cemento blanco grout
la pintura al agua latex paint	la base (ᶜla imprimación) primer	el papel estampado en relieve embossed paper	el solvente (ᶜel disolvente) solvent	el sellador (ᶜel sellante) sealant

---

el jardín • garden

los estilos de jardín • garden styles

el patio con jardín (ᶜ**la terraza ajardinada**)
patio garden

el jardín clásico | formal garden

el jardín campestre
cottage garden

el jardín de plantas herbáceas
herb garden

el jardín en la azotea
roof garden

la rocalla
rock garden

el patio
courtyard

el jardín acuático
water garden

la cesta colgante
hanging basket

la enredadera (ᶜ**la espaldera**) | trellis

la pérgola
arbor

la terraza
paving

la composta
(ᶜ el compost)
compost pile

el camino
path

el portón
(ᶜ la puerta)
gate

el parterre
flowerbed

el cobertizo
shed

el césped
lawn

el invernadero
greenhouse

el estanque
pond

la valla
fence

el seto
hedge

el arco
arch

el huerto
vegetable
garden

el arriate de plantas
herbáceas
herbaceous border

la tierra •
soil

**la capa superior
de la tierra**
topsoil

la arena
sand

la creta
chalk

el cieno
silt

la arcilla
clay

el entarimado
deck

la fuente | fountain

las plantas de jardín • garden plants

los tipos de plantas • types of plants

anual
annual

bienal
biennial

perenne
perennial

el bulbo
bulb

el helecho
fern

el junco
cattail

el bambú
bamboo

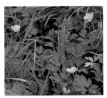
las malas hierbas
weeds

la hierba
herb

la planta acuática
water plant

el árbol
tree

de hoja caduca
deciduous

la palmera
palm

la conífera
conifer

de hoja perenne
evergreen

**as plantas podadas
con formas**
topiary

la planta alpestre
alpine

la planta suculenta
succulent

el cactus
cactus

la planta de maceta
potted plant

la planta de sombra
shade plant

**la planta
trepadora**
climber

**el arbusto de
flor**
flowering shrub

**la planta para
cubrir suelo**
ground cover

la planta trepadora
creeper

ornamental
ornamental

el pasto
(^C **el césped**)
grass

---

español • english

las herramientas de jardinería • gardening tools

la composta (^C**el abono compuesto**)
compost

las semillas
seeds

la harina de huesos
bone meal

la grava
gravel

el rastrillo para el pasto (^C**el césped**)
lawn rake

la pala
shovel

el trinche (^C**la horca**)
fork

la podadera de mango largo
long-handled shears

el rastrillo
rake

el azadón (^C**la azada**)
hoe

la bolsa para la hierba
grass bag

el motor
motor

el asa
handle

la cesta de jardinero
gardening basket

el protector
shield

el soporte
stand

la cortadora (^C**el guarnecedor**)
trimmer

la podadora (^C**el cortacésped**)
lawnmower

la carretilla
wheelbarrow

el trinche (^C**la horquilla**)
hand fork

la pala pequeña
trowel

la hoja
blade

las tijeras (^C**la cizalla**)
shears

la sierra de mano
hand saw

las podadoras (^C**las tijeras de podar**)
pruners

el semillero
seed tray

el pesticida
pesticide

los guantes de jardín
gardening gloves

el hilo de bramante
twine

las etiquetas
labels

el alambre
twist ties

las anillas
ring ties

las cañas
canes

la criba
sieve

la maceta
plant pot

las botas de goma
rubber boots

el riego • watering

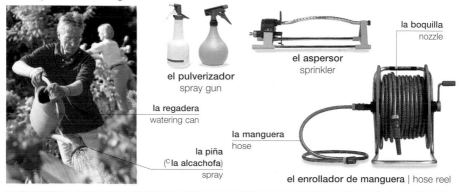

el pulverizador
spray gun

la regadera
watering can

la piña
(^C**la alcachofa**)
spray

el aspersor
sprinkler

la boquilla
nozzle

la manguera
hose

el enrollador de manguera | hose reel

la jardinería • gardening

el pasto
(^C el césped)
lawn

el seto
hedge

el parterre
flowerbed

la podadora
(^C el corta-
césped)
lawnmower

la estaca
stake

cortar el césped | mow (v)

poner césped
sod (v)

**hacer agujeros con la
trinche** (^C **la horquilla**)
spike (v)

rastrillar
rake (v)

podar
trim (v)

cavar
dig (v)

sembrar
sow (v)

abonar en la superficie
top-dress (v)

regar
water (v)

guiar
train (v)

quitar las flores muertas
deadhead (v)

rociar
spray (v)

la caña
cane

injertar
graft (v)

el esqueje
cutting

propagar
propagate (v)

podar
prune (v)

apuntalar
stake (v)

transplantar
transplant (v)

escardar
weed (v)

cubrir la tierra
mulch (v)

cosechar
harvest (v)

vocabulario • vocabulary

cultivar cultivate (v)	**diseñar** landscape (v)	**abonar** fertilize (v)	**cribar** sift (v)	**el drenaje** drainage	**el plantón** seedling	**el subsuelo** subsoil
cuidar tend (v)	**plantar en tiesto** pot (v)	**coger** pick (v)	**airear** aerate (v)	**orgánico** (ᶜ**biológico**) organic	**el abono** fertilizer	**el herbicida** weedkiller

los servicios
services

los servicios de emergencia • emergency services

la ambulancia • ambulance

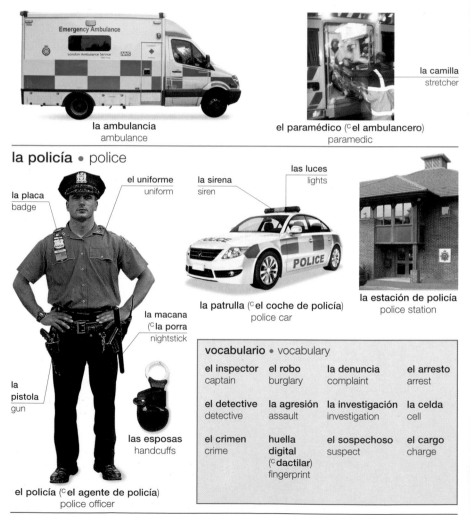

la camilla
stretcher

la ambulancia
ambulance

el paramédico (ᶜel ambulancero)
paramedic

la policía • police

la placa
badge

el uniforme
uniform

la sirena
siren

las luces
lights

la macana
(ᶜla porra
nightstick

la pistola
gun

la patrulla (ᶜel coche de policía)
police car

la estación de policía
police station

las esposas
handcuffs

el policía (ᶜel agente de policía)
police officer

vocabulario • vocabulary

el inspector captain	el robo burglary	la denuncia complaint	el arresto arrest
el detective detective	la agresión assault	la investigación investigation	la celda cell
el crimen crime	huella digital (ᶜdactilar) fingerprint	el sospechoso suspect	el cargo charge

los bomberos • fire department

el casco
helmet

el humo
smoke

la manguera
hose

la cesta
basket

el chorro
de agua
water jet

los bomberos
firefighters

el brazo
boom

la escalera
ladder

la cabina
cab

el incendio | fire

la estación (ᶜel
parque) de bomberos
fire station

la escalera (ᶜla salida)
de incendios
fire escape

el carro (ᶜel coche) de bomberos
fire engine

el detector de
humo
smoke alarm

la alarma contra
incendios
fire alarm

el hacha
ax

el extintor
fire extinguisher

la bomba (ᶜla
boca) de agua
hydrant

Necesito la policía/los bomberos/una ambulancia.
I need the police/fire department/ambulance

Hay un incendio en…
There's a fire at…

Ha habido un accidente.
There's been an accident.

¡Llame a la policía!
Call the police!

el banco • bank

el cliente
customer

la ventanilla
window

el cajero
teller

los folletos
brochures

el mostrador
counter

las fichas de
depósito (ᶜlas
hojas de ingreso)
deposit slips

la tarjeta de débito
debit card

la matriz
stub

el número de
cuenta
account number

la firma
signature

la cantidad
amount

el gerente del banco
(ᶜel director de banco)
branch manager

la tarjeta de crédito
credit card

el talonario de cheques
checkbook

el cheque
check

---

vocabulario • vocabulary

los ahorros savings	la hipoteca mortgage	el pago payment	depositar (ᶜingresar) deposit (v)	la cuenta corriente checking account
el sobregiro (ᶜel descubierto) overdraft	la tasa (ᶜel tipo) de interés interest rate	la hoja de reintegro withdrawal slip	el pin PIN	la cuenta de ahorros savings account
el préstamo loan	los impuestos tax	el débito directo (ᶜla domiciliación bancaria) automatic payment	la transferencia bancaria bank transfer	la comisión bancaria bank charge

---

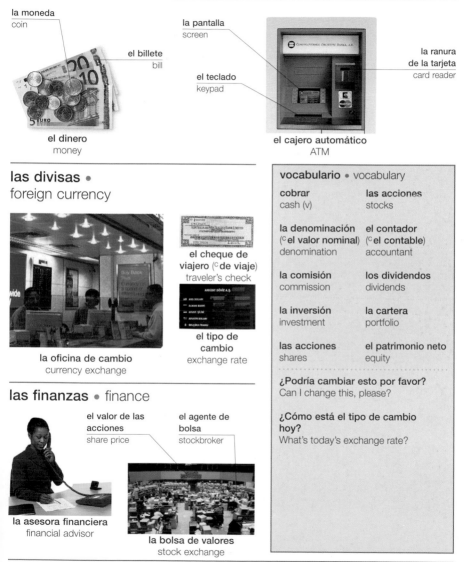

la moneda
coin

el billete
bill

el dinero
money

la pantalla
screen

el teclado
keypad

la ranura
de la tarjeta
card reader

el cajero automático
ATM

las divisas •
foreign currency

la oficina de cambio
currency exchange

el cheque de
viajero (^cde viaje)
traveler's check

el tipo de
cambio
exchange rate

las finanzas • finance

el valor de las
acciones
share price

el agente de
bolsa
stockbroker

la asesora financiera
financial advisor

la bolsa de valores
stock exchange

vocabulario • vocabulary

cobrar
cash (v)

la denominación
(^cel valor nominal)
denomination

la comisión
commission

la inversión
investment

las acciones
shares

las acciones
stocks

el contador
(^cel contable)
accountant

los dividendos
dividends

la cartera
portfolio

el patrimonio neto
equity

¿Podría cambiar esto por favor?
Can I change this, please?

¿Cómo está el tipo de cambio
hoy?
What's today's exchange rate?

las comunicaciones • communications

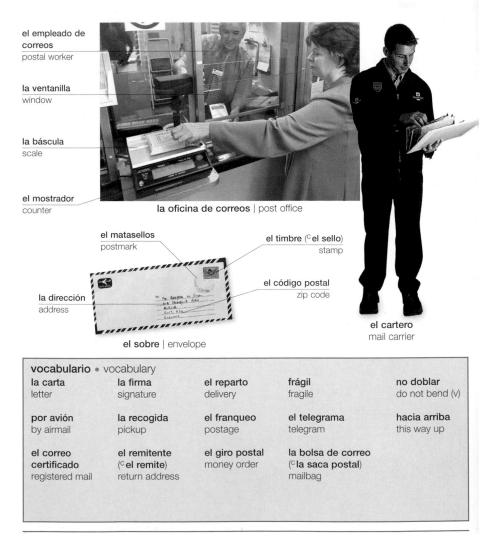

el empleado de correos
postal worker

la ventanilla
window

la báscula
scale

el mostrador
counter

la oficina de correos | post office

el matasellos
postmark

el timbre (ᶜel sello)
stamp

la dirección
address

el código postal
zip code

el cartero
mail carrier

el sobre | envelope

---

vocabulario • vocabulary

la carta letter	la firma signature	el reparto delivery	frágil fragile	no doblar do not bend (v)
por avión by airmail	la recogida pickup	el franqueo postage	el telegrama telegram	hacia arriba this way up
el correo certificado registered mail	el remitente (ᶜel remite) return address	el giro postal money order	la bolsa de correo (ᶜla saca postal) mailbag	

---

español • english

el buzón
mailbox

el buzón
letter slot

el paquete
package

la mensajería
courier

el teléfono • telephone

el auricular
handset

la base
base station

el teléfono inalámbrico
cordless phone

la contestadora
(ᶜel contestador
automático)
answering machine

el videoteléfono
video phone

la cabina telefónica
phone booth

**el teléfono
inteligente**
smartphone

el teléfono móvil
cell phone

el teclado
keypad

el auricular
receiver

las monedas devueltas
coin return

el teléfono público
payphone

vocabulario • vocabulary

la información telefónica directory assistance	**el mensaje de texto (SMS)** text (SMS)	**ocupado** (ᶜ**comunicando**) busy	**¿Me podría dar el número de...?** Can you give me the number for...?
la llamada por cobrar (ᶜ**a cobro revertido**) collect call	**el mensaje de voz** voice message	**desconectado** (ᶜ**apagado**) disconnected	**¿Cuál es el prefijo de larga distancia para llamar a...?** What is the area code for...?
marcar dial (v)	**el operador** operator	**la clave de acceso** passcode	**¡Mándame un mensaje de texto!** Text me!
contestar answer (v)	**la aplicación** app		

el hotel • hotel
el lobby (ᶜel vestíbulo) • lobby

el huésped
guest

la llave de la
habitación
room key

los mensajes
messages

la casilla
pigeonhole

la recepcionista
receptionist

el registro
register

el mostrador
counter

la recepción | reception

el botones
porter

el equipaje
luggage

el diablito
(ᶜel carrito)
cart

el elevador (ᶜel ascensor)
elevator

**el número de la
habitación**
room number

los habitaciones • rooms

**la habitación sencilla
(ᶜindividual)**
single room

la habitación doble
double room

**la habitación con dos
camas individuales**
twin room

el baño (ᶜel cuarto de
baño) **privado**
private bathroom

los servicios • services

la charola (^Cla bandeja) del desayuno
breakfast tray

**el servicio de
limpieza**
maid service

**el servicio de
lavandería**
laundry service

el servicio de habitaciones | room service

el minibar
minibar

el restaurante
restaurant

el gimnasio
gym

la piscina
swimming pool

---

vocabulario • vocabulary

la pensión completa
all meals included

la media pensión
some meals included

**la habitación con
desayuno incluido**
bed and breakfast

¿Tiene alguna habitación libre?
Do you have any vacancies?

**Tengo una reservación
(^Creserva).**
I have a reservation.

**Quiero una habitación
sencilla (^Cindividual).**
I'd like a single room.

**Quiero una habitación para
tres noches.**
I'd like a room for three nights.

¿Cuánto cuesta la habitación por día?
What is the charge per night?

**¿Cuándo tengo que dejar la
habitación?**
When do I have to check out?

---

español • english

101

las compras
shopping

el centro comercial • shopping center

el atrio
atrium

el letrero
sign

el elevador
(^C el ascensor)
elevator

el segundo piso
(^C la segunda planta)
third floor

el primer piso
(^C la primera planta)
second floor

la escalera eléctrica
(^C mecánica)
escalator

la planta baja
ground floor

el cliente
customer

---

vocabulario • vocabulary

el departamento (^C la sección) de zapatería
shoe department

la sección de niños
children's department

el departamento (^C la sección) de equipajes
luggage department

el servicio al cliente
customer services

el directorio
store directory

el vendedor
(^C el dependiente)
salesclerk

el cuarto para cambiar a los bebés
baby changing room

los probadores
fitting rooms

los baños (^C los aseos)
restroom

¿Cuánto cuesta esto?
How much is this?

¿Puedo cambiar esto?
May I exchange this?

---

los grandes almacenes • department store

la ropa de caballero
menswear

la ropa de dama
(ᶜ **de señora**)
womenswear

la lencería
lingerie

la perfumería
perfumes

los cosméticos
(ᶜ **los productos de belleza**)
cosmetics

los blancos (ᶜ **la ropa de hogar**)
linens

el mobiliario para el hogar
home furnishings

la mercería
notions

los artículos de cocina
(ᶜ **el menaje de hogar**)
kitchenware

la porcelana
china

los aparatos eléctricos
electronics

la iluminación
lighting

los artículos deportivos
sportswear

la juguetería
toys

la papelería
stationery

los abarrotes
(ᶜ **el supermercado**)
groceries

el supermercado • supermarket

el pasillo
aisle

el estante
shelf

la banda (^C la cinta)
transportadora
conveyer belt

el cajero
cashier

las ofertas
specials

la caja | checkout

el cliente
customer

la caja
cash register

la bolsa
de la compra
shopping bag

la compra
groceries

el asa
handle

el código de barras
bar code

el carrito (^C el carro)
grocery cart

la canasta (^C la cesta)
basket

el escáner
scanner

la panadería
bakery

los lácteos
dairy

los cereales
breakfast cereals

las conservas
canned food

la dulcería
(ᶜ**los golosinas**)
candy

la verdura
vegetables

la fruta
fruit

la carne y las aves
meat and poultry

el pescado
fish

los comestibles finos
deli

los congelados
frozen food

los platos preparados
prepared food

las bebidas
drinks

los productos de limpieza
household products

los artículos de aseo
toiletries

los artículos para el bebé
baby products

los electrodomésticos
electrical goods

la comida para animales
pet food

las revistas | magazines

la farmacia • drugstore

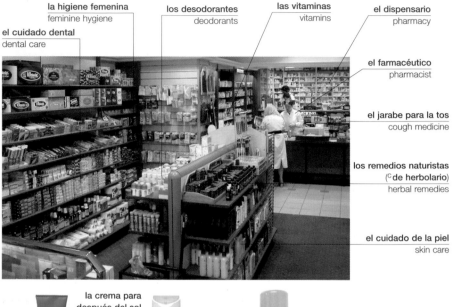

la higiene femenina
feminine hygiene

el cuidado dental
dental care

los desodorantes
deodorants

las vitaminas
vitamins

el dispensario
pharmacy

el farmacéutico
pharmacist

el jarabe para la tos
cough medicine

los remedios naturistas
(ᶜ de herbolario)
herbal remedies

el cuidado de la piel
skin care

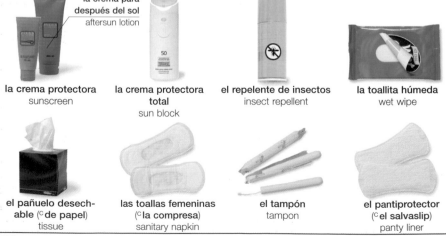

**la crema para
después del sol**
aftersun lotion

la crema protectora
sunscreen

**la crema protectora
total**
sun block

el repelente de insectos
insect repellent

la toallita húmeda
wet wipe

**el pañuelo desech-
able** (ᶜ de papel)
tissue

las toallas femeninas
(ᶜ la compresa)
sanitary napkin

el tampón
tampon

el pantiprotector
(ᶜ el salvaslip)
panty liner

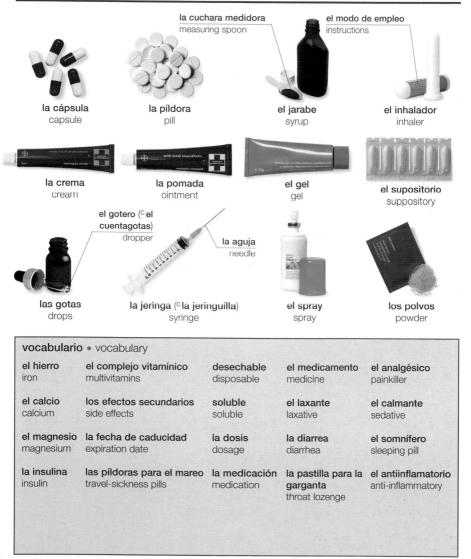

la cuchara medidora
measuring spoon

el modo de empleo
instructions

la cápsula
capsule

la píldora
pill

el jarabe
syrup

el inhalador
inhaler

la crema
cream

la pomada
ointment

el gel
gel

el supositorio
suppository

el gotero (ᶜ **el cuentagotas**)
dropper

la aguja
needle

las gotas
drops

la jeringa (ᶜ **la jeringuilla**)
syringe

el spray
spray

los polvos
powder

---

vocabulario • vocabulary

el hierro iron	**el complejo vitamínico** multivitamins	**desechable** disposable	**el medicamento** medicine	**el analgésico** painkiller
el calcio calcium	**los efectos secundarios** side effects	**soluble** soluble	**el laxante** laxative	**el calmante** sedative
el magnesio magnesium	**la fecha de caducidad** expiration date	**la dosis** dosage	**la diarrea** diarrhea	**el somnífero** sleeping pill
la insulina insulin	**las píldoras para el mareo** travel-sickness pills	**la medicación** medication	**la pastilla para la garganta** throat lozenge	**el antiinflamatorio** anti-inflammatory

la florería (ᶜ la floristería) • florist

las flores
flowers

la azucena
lily

la acacia
acacia

el clavel
carnation

la maceta
potted plant

la gladiola
(ᶜ el gladiolo)
gladiolus

el iris
iris

la margarita
daisy

el crisantemo
chrysanthemum

la nube
(ᶜ la gypsofila)
gypsophila

el alhelí
stocks

la gerbera
gerbera

el follaje
foliage

la rosa
rose

la fresia
freesia

el florero (ᶜel jarrón)
vase

la orquídea
orchid

la peonía
peony

el ramo
bunch

el tallo
stem

el narciso
daffodil

el capullo
bud

la envoltura
(ᶜel envoltorio)
wrapping

el tulipán | tulip

los arreglos • arrangements

la cinta
ribbon

el ramo
bouquet

las flores secas
dried flowers

el popurrí | potpourri

la corona | wreath

la guirnalda
garland

vocabulario • vocabulary

**¿Me da un ramo de…
por favor?**
Can I have a bunch
of… please?

¿Me los puede envolver?
Can I have them wrapped?

¿Puedo poner un mensaje?
Can I attach a message?

¿Los puede enviar a…?
Can you send them to…?

**¿Cuánto tiempo durarán
éstos?**
How long will these last?

¿Huelen?
Are they fragrant?

los tabacos y las revistas (^Cel vendedor de periódicos) •
newsstand

los cigarros
(^Clos cigarrillos)
cigarettes

la cajetilla de cigarros
(^Cel paquete de tabaco)
pack of cigarettes

los timbres
(^Clos sellos)
stamps

la tarjeta postal
postcard

la historieta (^Cel tebeo)
comic book

la revista
magazine

el periódico
newspaper

fumar • smoking

el tubo
stem

la cazoleta
bowl

el tabaco
tobacco

el encendedor (^Cel mechero)
lighter

la pipa
pipe

el puro
cigar

la dulcería • candy store

la caja de chocolates
(ᶜde bombones)
box of chocolates

la barrita
snack bar

las papas
(ᶜpatatas) fritas
potato chips

la dulcería (ᶜla tienda de golosinas) | candy store

vocabulario • vocabulary

el chocolate
de leche
(ᶜel chocolate
con leche)
milk chocolate

el chocolate
negro
dark chocolate

el chocolate
blanco
white chocolate

los dulces
(ᶜlas golosinas)
a granel
pick and mix

el caramelo
caramel

la trufa
truffle

la galleta
cookie

los dulces (ᶜlas golosinas) • confectionery

el chocolate
(ᶜel bombón)
chocolate

**la tablilla (ᶜla tableta)
de chocolate**
chocolate bar

los caramelos duros
hard candy

la paleta (ᶜla piruleta)
lollipop

el toffee
toffee

el turrón
nougat

el malvarisco (ᶜla nube)
marshmallow

la pastilla de menta
mint

el chicle
chewing gum

el caramelo blando
jellybean

la gomita (ᶜla gominola)
gumdrop

el regaliz
licorice

las otras tiendas • other stores

la panadería
bakery

la confitería
pastry shop

la carnicería
butcher shop

la pescadería
fish counter

la verdulería
produce stand

los abarrotes
(ᶜ **la tienda de comestible**)
grocery store

la zapatería
shoe store

la ferretería
hardware store

**la tienda de
antigüedades**
antique store

la tienda de regalos
(ᶜ **de artículos de regalo**)
gift shop

la agencia de viajes
travel agency

la joyería
jewelry store

la librería
bookstore

la tienda de discos
record store

la tienda de licores
liquor store

la tienda de mascotas
(^C**la pajarería**)
pet store

la mueblería
(^C**la tienda de muebles**)
furniture store

la boutique
boutique

vocabulario • vocabulary

el vivero
garden center

la tienda de fotografía
camera store

la tienda naturista
(^C**la herboristería**)
health food store

la tienda de artículos usados
secondhand store

la lavandería
laundromat

la tintorería
dry cleaner

la agencia inmobiliaria
real estate office

la galería de arte
(^C**la tienda de arte**)
art supply store

la sastrería
tailor shop

la estética (^C**la peluquería**)
salon

el mercado | market

los alimentos
food

la carne • meat

el cordero
lamb

el carnicero
butcher

el gancho
meat hook

la báscula
(ᶜ el peso)
scale

el afilador
knife sharpener

el tocino (ᶜ el bacon)
bacon

las salchichas
sausages

el hígado
liver

vocabulario • vocabulary

el cerdo pork	**el venado** venison	**las asaduras** variety meat	**de granja** free range	**la carne roja** red meat
la vaca beef	**el conejo** rabbit	**curado** cured	**la carne blanca** white meat	**la carne magra** lean meat
la ternera veal	**la lengua** tongue	**ahumado** smoked	**orgánico** (ᶜ**biológico**) organic	**el fiambre** cooked meat

los cortes • cuts

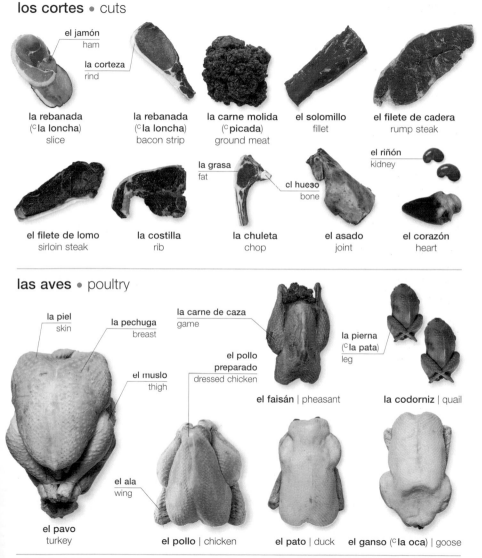

la rebanada
(^c**la loncha**)
slice

el jamón
ham

la corteza
rind

la rebanada
(^c**la loncha**)
bacon strip

la carne molida
(^c**picada**)
ground meat

el solomillo
fillet

el filete de cadera
rump steak

el filete de lomo
sirloin steak

la costilla
rib

la grasa
fat

el hueso
bone

la chuleta
chop

el asado
joint

el riñón
kidney

el corazón
heart

las aves • poultry

la piel
skin

la pechuga
breast

el muslo
thigh

la carne de caza
game

**el pollo
preparado**
dressed chicken

la pierna
(^c**la pata**)
leg

el faisán | pheasant

la codorniz | quail

el ala
wing

el pavo
turkey

el pollo | chicken

el pato | duck

el ganso (^c**la oca**) | goose

el pescado • fish

los camarones pelados
(ᶜ las gambas peladas)
peeled shrimp

el salmonete
red mullet

los filetes
de mero
halibut fillets

la trucha arco iris
rainbow trout

el hielo
ice

las aletas de
raya
skate wings

la pescadería
fish counter

el rape
monkfish

la caballa
mackerel

la trucha
trout

el pez espada
swordfish

el lenguado
Dover sole

la platija
lemon sole

el abadejo
haddock

la sardina
sardine

la raya
skate

la pescadilla
whiting

la lubina
sea bass

el salmón | salmon

el bacalao
cod

el besugo
sea bream

el atún
tuna

el marisco • seafood

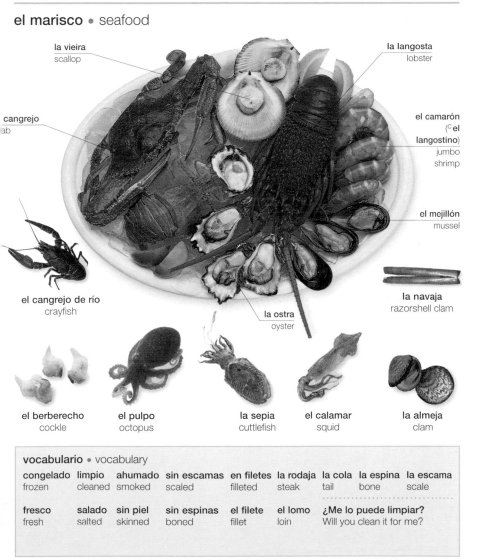

la vieira
scallop

la langosta
lobster

cangrejo
ab

el camarón
(C el
langostino)
jumbo
shrimp

el mejillón
mussel

el cangrejo de río
crayfish

la ostra
oyster

la navaja
razorshell clam

el berberecho
cockle

el pulpo
octopus

la sepia
cuttlefish

el calamar
squid

la almeja
clam

vocabulario • vocabulary

congelado	limpio	ahumado	sin escamas	en filetes	la rodaja	la cola	la espina	la escama
frozen	cleaned	smoked	scaled	filleted	steak	tail	bone	scale

fresco	salado	sin piel	sin espinas	el filete	el lomo	¿Me lo puede limpiar?
fresh	salted	skinned	boned	fillet	loin	Will you clean it for me?

las verduras 1 • vegetables 1

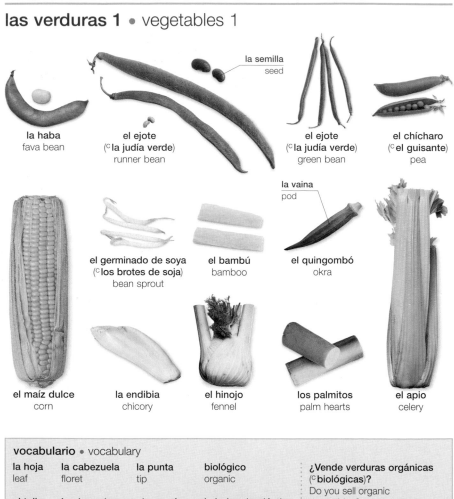

la semilla
seed

la haba
fava bean

el ejote
(ᶜla judía verde)
runner bean

el ejote
(ᶜla judía verde)
green bean

el chícharo
(ᶜel guisante)
pea

la vaina
pod

el germinado de soya
(ᶜlos brotes de soja)
bean sprout

el bambú
bamboo

el quingombó
okra

el maíz dulce
corn

la endibia
chicory

el hinojo
fennel

los palmitos
palm hearts

el apio
celery

---

vocabulario • vocabulary

la hoja leaf	**la cabezuela** floret	**la punta** tip	**biológico** organic	**¿Vende verduras orgánicas** (ᶜ**biológicas)?** Do you sell organic vegetables?
el tallo stalk	**la almendra** kernel	**el corazón** (ᶜ**el centro)** heart	**la bolsa de plástico** plastic bag	**¿Son productos locales?** Are these grown locally?

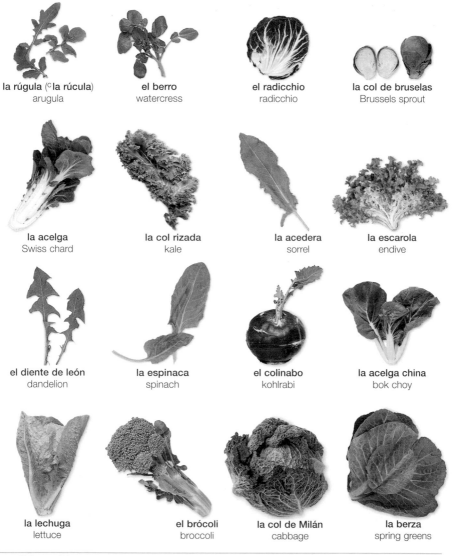

la rúgula (^C**la rúcula**)
arugula

el berro
watercress

el radicchio
radicchio

la col de bruselas
Brussels sprout

la acelga
Swiss chard

la col rizada
kale

la acedera
sorrel

la escarola
endive

el diente de león
dandelion

la espinaca
spinach

el colinabo
kohlrabi

la acelga china
bok choy

la lechuga
lettuce

el brócoli
broccoli

la col de Milán
cabbage

la berza
spring greens

las verduras 2 • vegetables 2

el nabo
turnip

la alcachofa
artichoke

el rábano
radish

la coliflor
cauliflower

el espárrago
asparagus

la papa
(ᶜla patata)
potato

la calabacita
(ᶜel calabacín)
gigante
squash

la cebolla
onion

el pimiento
pepper

la chilaca
(ᶜla guindilla)
chili pepper

el maíz
sweetcorn

vocabulario • vocabulary

la mandioca cassava	**el apio-nabo** celeriac	**congelado** frozen	**amargo** bitter	**¿Me da un kilo de papas** (ᶜ**patatas), por favor?** Can I have one kilo of potatoes, please?
la zanahoria carrot	**la raíz del taro** taro root	**crudo** raw	**firme** firm	
el fruto del pan breadfruit	**la castaña de agua** water chestnut	**picante** hot (spicy)	**la pulpa** flesh	**¿Cuánto vale el kilo?** What's the price per kilo?
la papa (ᶜ**la** **patata) nueva** new potato	**el jitomate** (ᶜ el **tomate) cherry** cherry tomato	**dulce** sweet	**la raíz** root	**¿Cómo se llaman?** What are those called?

el camote
(^C **el boniato**)
sweet potato

el ñame
yam

el betabel
(^C **la remolacha**)
beet

el nabo
(^C **el nabo sueco**)
rutabaga

el topinambur
Jerusalem
artichoke

el rábano picante
horseradish

la chirivía
parsnip

el jengibre
ginger

la berenjena
eggplant

el jitomate
(^C **el tomate**)
tomato

el cebollín
(^C **la cebolleta**)
scallion

el puerro
leek

el chalote
shallot

el ajo
garlic

el diente
clove

la trufa
truffle

la seta
mushroom

el pepino
cucumber

la calabacita
(^C **el calabacín**)
zucchini

la calabaza
butternut squash

la calabaza
bellota
acorn squash

la calabaza
pumpkin

la fruta 1 • fruit 1

los cítricos • citrus fruit

la naranja
orange

la mandarina clementina
clementine

el ugli
ugli fruit

la piel (ᶜ**la médula**)
pith

la toronja (ᶜ**el pomelo**)
grapefruit

el gajo
segment

la mandarina satsuma
satsuma

la mandarina
tangerine

la cáscara
zest

la lima
lime

el limón
lemon

la naranja china (ᶜ**el kumquat**)
kumquat

la fruta con hueso • stone fruit

el durazno
(ᶜ**el melocotón**)
peach

la nectarina
nectarine

el chabacano
(ᶜ**el albaricoque**)
apricot

la ciruela
plum

la cereza
cherry

la manzana
apple

la pera
pear

el frutero (ᶜ**la cesta de fruta**) | basket of fruit

las bayas y los melones • berries and melons

la fresa
strawberry

la frambuesa
raspberry

el melón
melon

la uva
grapes

la zarzamora (^C**la mora**)
blackberry

la grosella
redcurrant

la cáscara
(^C**la corteza**)
rind

el arándano rojo
cranberry

la grosella negra
black currant

la semilla
(^C**la pepita**)
seed

el arándano
blueberry

la grosella blanca
white currant

la pulpa
flesh

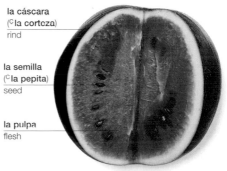
la sandía
watermelon

la frambuesa Logan
loganberry

el capulín
(^C**la grosella espinosa**)
gooseberry

vocabulario • vocabulary

el ruibarbo rhubarb	**amargo** sour	**fresco** crisp	**el corazón** core	**¿Están maduros?** Are they ripe?
la fibra fiber	**fresco** fresh	**podrido** rotten	**la pulpa** pulp	**¿Puedo probar uno?** Can I try one?
dulce sweet	**jugoso** juicy	**el jugo** (^C**el zumo**) juice	**sin semillas** (^C**pepitas**) seedless	**¿Hasta cuándo durarán?** How long will they keep?

la fruta 2 • fruit 2

el mango
mango

la piña
pineapple

el aguacate
avocado

la papaya
papaya

el melocotón
peach

el lichi
lychee

el capulín
(ᶜel alquequenje)
Cape gooseberry

el kiwi
kiwifruit

la semilla
seed

la piel
peel

el membrillo
quince

el maracuyá
passion fruit

el plátano
banana

la guayaba
guava

la granada
pomegranate

el caqui
persimmon

la feijoa
feijoa

la tuna
(ᶜ**el higo chumbo**)
prickly pear

la carambola
star fruit

el tamarillo
tamarillo

los frutos seco • nuts and dried fruit

el piñón
pine nut

el pistache
(c **el pistacho**)
pistachio

la nuez de la India
(c **el anacardo**)
cashew

el cacahuete
peanut

la avellana
hazelnut

la nuez de Brasil
Brazil nut

la nuez
(c **la pacana**)
pecan

la almendra
almond

la nuez de Castilla
(c **la nuez**) | walnut

la castaña
chestnut

la macadamia
macadamia

el higo
fig

el dátil
date

la ciruela pasa
prune

la cáscara
shell

la pulpa
flesh

la pasa sultana
sultana

la pasa
raisin

la pasa de Corinto
currant

el coco
coconut

vocabulario • vocabulary

verde green	**duro** hard	**la almendra** kernel	**salado** salted	**tostado** roasted	**las frutas tropicales** tropical fruit	**pelado** shelled
maduro ripe	**blando** soft	**desecado** desiccated	**crudo** raw	**de temporada** seasonal	**la fruta escarchada** candied fruit	**entero** whole

los granos y las legumbres • grains and pulses

los granos • grains

el trigo
wheat

la avena
oats

la cebada
barley

el mijo
millet

el maíz
corn

la quinoa
quinoa

vocabulario • vocabulary		
la semilla seed	**fresco** fresh	**integral** whole-grain
la cáscara husk	**perfumado** fragranced	**largo** long-grain
el grano kernel	**los cereales** cereal	**corto** short-grain
seco dry	**poner a remojo** soak (v)	**de fácil cocción** quick cooking

el arroz • rice

los granos procesados • processed grains

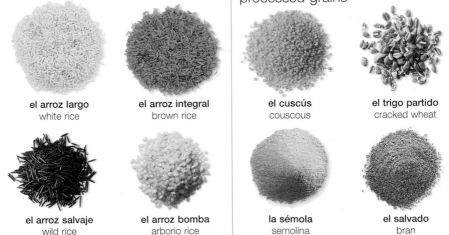

el arroz largo
white rice

el arroz integral
brown rice

el arroz salvaje
wild rice

el arroz bomba
arborio rice

el cuscús
couscous

el trigo partido
cracked wheat

la sémola
semolina

el salvado
bran

130

los frijoles y los chícharos (^Clas legumbres) • beans and peas

el frijol blanco
(^C**la alubia blanca**)
butter beans

el frijol blanco chico
(^C**la alubia blanca**
pequeña) | haricot beans

el frijol rojo
(^C**la alubia roja**)
red kidney beans

el frijol morado
(^C**la alubia morada**)
adzuki beans

las habas
fava beans

la semilla de soja
soybeans

el frijol (^C**la alubia**)
de ojo negro
black-eyed peas

el frijol pinto
(^C**la alubia pinta**)
pinto beans

el frijol mung
(^C**la alubia mung**)
mung beans

el frijol flageolet
(^C**la alubia flageolet**)
flageolet beans

la lenteja
castellana
brown lentils

la lenteja roja
red lentils

los chícharos
(^C**los guisantes tiernos**)
green peas

los garbanzos
chickpeas

los chícharos secos
(^C**los guisantes secos**)
split peas

las semillas • seeds

la pepita (^C**la**
pipa) de
calabaza
pumpkin seed

la semilla de
mostaza (^C**la**
mostaza en grano)
mustard seed

el carvi
caraway

la semilla de
sésamo
sesame seed

la semilla de girasol (^C**la pipa**
de girasol) | sunflower seed

las hierbas y las especias • herbs and spices

las especias • spices

la vainilla
vanilla

la nuez moscada
nutmeg

la macis
mace

la cúrcuma
turmeric

el comino
cumin

el ramillete aromático
bouquet garni

la pimienta de Jamaica
allspice

la pimienta en grano
peppercorn

el heno griego
fenugreek

el chile piquín
(ᶜ **la guindilla**)
chili powder

entero	machacado
whole	crushed

el azafrán
saffron

el cardamono
cardamom

el curry en polvo
curry powder

molido
ground

el pimentón
paprika

las hojuelas
(ᶜ**laminado**)
flakes

el ajo
garlic

las hierbas • herbs

las rajas
(ᶜ las ramas)
sticks

la canela
cinnamon

la citronela
lemon grass

los clavos
cloves

el anís estrellado
star anise

el jengibre
ginger

el hinojo
fennel

las semillas de hinojo
fennel seeds

el cebollino
chives

el estragón
tarragon

el orégano
oregano

la menta
mint

la mejorana
marjoram

el cilantro
cilantro

el laurel
bay leaf

el tomillo
thyme

la albahaca
basil

el eneldo
dill

el perejil
parsley

la salvia
sage

el romero
rosemary

los alimentos embotellados •
bottled foods

el aceite de nueces
walnut oil

el aceite de almendras
almond oil

el aceite de semillas de uva
grapeseed oil

el corcho
cork

el aceite de girasol
sunflower oil

el aceite de sésamo
sesame seed oil

el aceite de avellanas
hazelnut oil

el aceite de oliva
olive oil

las hierbas
herbs

el aceite aromatizado
flavored oil

los aceites
oils

las conservas dulces • sweet spreads

el tarro
jar

el panal
honeycomb

la miel cristalizada
(^Ccompacta)
set honey

la crema de limón
lemon curd

la mermelada de frambuesa
raspberry jam

la mermelada de naranja
marmalade

la miel líquida
clear honey

la miel de maple
(^Cel jarabe de arce)
maple syrup

las salsas y los condimentos •
sauces and condiments

la botella
bottle

el vinagre de sidra
cider vinegar

el vinagre
balsámico
balsamic vinegar

la mostaza
inglesa
English mustard

la mayonesa
mayonnaise

la catsup
(^{C} el ketchup)
ketchup

la mostaza
francesa
French mustard

el chutney
chutney

el vinagre de malta
malt vinegar

el vinagre de vino
wine vinegar

el vinagre
vinegar

la salsa
sauce

la mostaza en
grano
whole-grain
mustard

---

el tarro hermético
canning jar

la crema de
cacahuete
peanut butter

el chocolate para
untar
chocolate spread

la fruta en
conserva
preserved fruit

vocabulario • vocabulary

el aceite
vegetal
vegetable oil

el aceite de
colza
canola oil

el aceite de
maíz
corn oil

el aceite de
presión en frío
cold-pressed oil

el aceite de
cacahuete
peanut oil

---

los productos lácteos • dairy products

el queso • cheese

la corteza
rind

el queso semicurado
semi-hard cheese

el queso rallado
grated cheese

el queso curado
hard cheese

el queso cremoso semicurado
semi-soft cheese

el requesón
cottage cheese

el queso cremoso
cream cheese

el queso azul
blue cheese

el queso cremoso
soft cheese

el queso fresco | fresh cheese

la leche • milk

la leche entera
whole milk

la leche semidescremada
(ᶜsemidesnatada)
reduced-fat milk

la leche descremada
(ᶜdesnatada)
skim milk

el cartón de leche
milk carton

la leche de cabra
goat's milk

la leche condensada
condensed milk

la leche de vaca | cow's milk

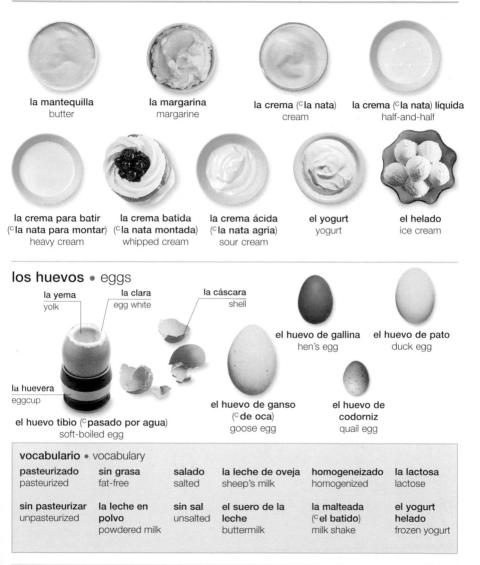

la mantequilla
butter

la margarina
margarine

la crema (ᶜla nata)
cream

la crema (ᶜla nata) **líquida**
half-and-half

la crema para batir
(ᶜla nata para montar)
heavy cream

la crema batida
(ᶜla nata montada)
whipped cream

la crema ácida
(ᶜla nata agria)
sour cream

el yogurt
yogurt

el helado
ice cream

los huevos • eggs

la yema
yolk

la clara
egg white

la cáscara
shell

el huevo de gallina
hen's egg

el huevo de pato
duck egg

la huevera
eggcup

el huevo tibio (ᶜpasado por agua)
soft-boiled egg

el huevo de ganso
(ᶜde oca)
goose egg

el huevo de codorniz
quail egg

vocabulario • vocabulary

pasteurizado pasteurized	**sin grasa** fat-free	**salado** salted	**la leche de oveja** sheep's milk	**homogeneizado** homogenized	**la lactosa** lactose
sin pasteurizar unpasteurized	**la leche en polvo** powdered milk	**sin sal** unsalted	**el suero de la leche** buttermilk	**la malteada** (ᶜel batido) milk shake	**el yogurt helado** frozen yogurt

el pan y las harinas • breads and flours

el pan de caja
(^cde molde)
sliced bread

las semillas de
amapola
poppy seeds

el pan de centeno
rye bread

la baguette
baguette

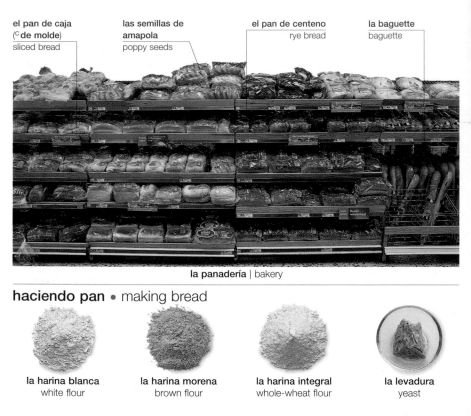

la panadería | bakery

haciendo pan • making bread

la harina blanca
white flour

la harina morena
brown flour

la harina integral
whole-wheat flour

la levadura
yeast

la masa
dough

cernir (^c**cribar**) | sift (v)

mezclar | mix (v)

amasar | knead (v)

hornear | bake (v)

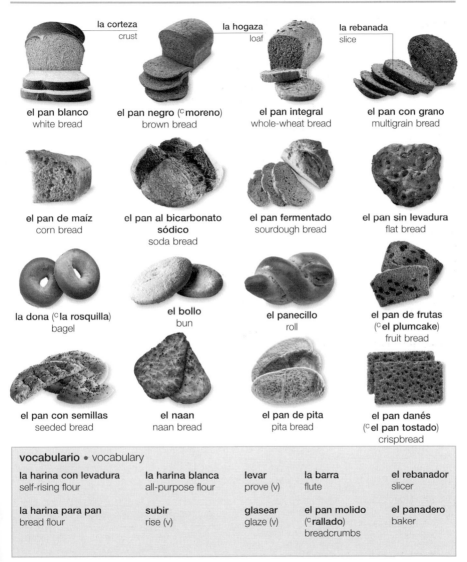

la corteza
crust

la hogaza
loaf

la rebanada
slice

el pan blanco
white bread

el pan negro (ᶜ**moreno**)
brown bread

el pan integral
whole-wheat bread

el pan con grano
multigrain bread

el pan de maíz
corn bread

**el pan al bicarbonato
sódico**
soda bread

el pan fermentado
sourdough bread

el pan sin levadura
flat bread

la dona (ᶜ**la rosquilla**)
bagel

el bollo
bun

el panecillo
roll

el pan de frutas
(ᶜ**el plumcake**)
fruit bread

el pan con semillas
seeded bread

el naan
naan bread

el pan de pita
pita bread

el pan danés
(ᶜ**el pan tostado**)
crispbread

---

vocabulario • vocabulary

la harina con levadura self-rising flour	**la harina blanca** all-purpose flour	**levar** prove (v)	**la barra** flute	**el rebanador** slicer
la harina para pan bread flour	**subir** rise (v)	**glasear** glaze (v)	**el pan molido** (ᶜ**rallado**) breadcrumbs	**el panadero** baker

la repostería • cakes and desserts

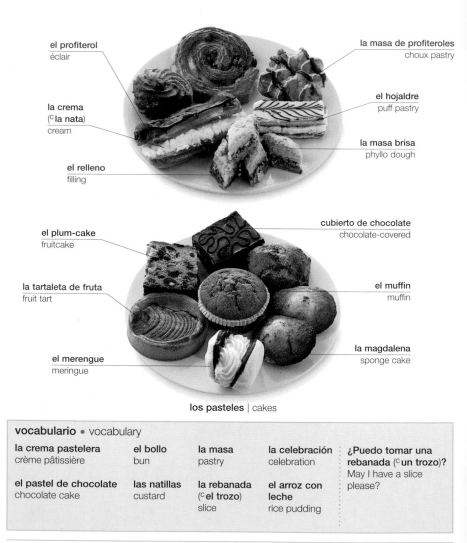

el profiterol
éclair

la masa de profiteroles
choux pastry

la crema
(^Cla nata)
cream

el hojaldre
puff pastry

la masa brisa
phyllo dough

el relleno
filling

el plum-cake
fruitcake

cubierto de chocolate
chocolate-covered

la tartaleta de fruta
fruit tart

el muffin
muffin

el merengue
meringue

la magdalena
sponge cake

los pasteles | cakes

vocabulario • vocabulary

la crema pastelera crème pâtissière	**el bollo** bun	**la masa** pastry	**la celebración** celebration	**¿Puedo tomar una rebanada (^Cun trozo)?** May I have a slice please?
el pastel de chocolate chocolate cake	**las natillas** custard	**la rebanada** (^C**el trozo**) slice	**el arroz con leche** rice pudding	

las soletillas
ladyfinger

los chips (ᶜel trocito)
de chocolate
chocolate chip

el postre de soletillas,
gelatina de frutas y
crema (ᶜel postre de
soletillas, gelatina de
frutas y nata)
trifle

la florentina
Florentine

las galletas | cookies

el mousse (ᶜla mousse)
mousse

el sorbete
sherbet

el pastel de crema (ᶜnata)
cream pie

el flan
crème caramel

los pasteles para celebraciones (c las tartas para celebraciones) • celebration cakes

el último piso
top tier

el listón
(ᶜla cinta)
ribbon

la decoración
decoration

las velas de
cumpleaños
birthday candles

apagar
blow out (v)

el primer piso
bottom tier

la alcorza
frosting

el mazapán
marzipan

el pastel de bodas (ᶜla tarta nupcial)
wedding cake

el pastel (ᶜla tarta) **de cumpleaños** | birthday cake

la charcutería • delicatessen

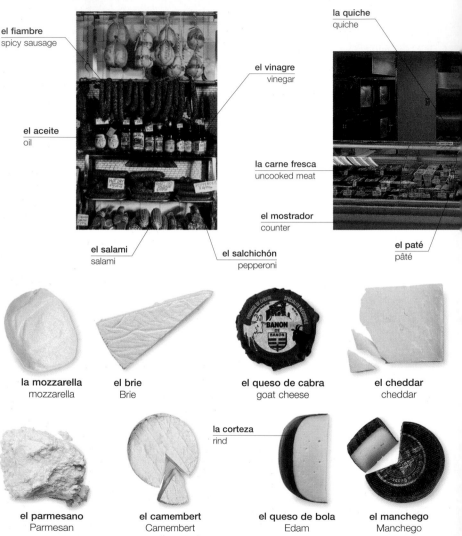

el fiambre
spicy sausage

la quiche
quiche

el vinagre
vinegar

el aceite
oil

la carne fresca
uncooked meat

el mostrador
counter

el salami
salami

el salchichón
pepperoni

el paté
pâté

la mozzarella
mozzarella

el brie
Brie

el queso de cabra
goat cheese

el cheddar
cheddar

el parmesano
Parmesan

el camembert
Camembert

la corteza
rind

el queso de bola
Edam

el manchego
Manchego

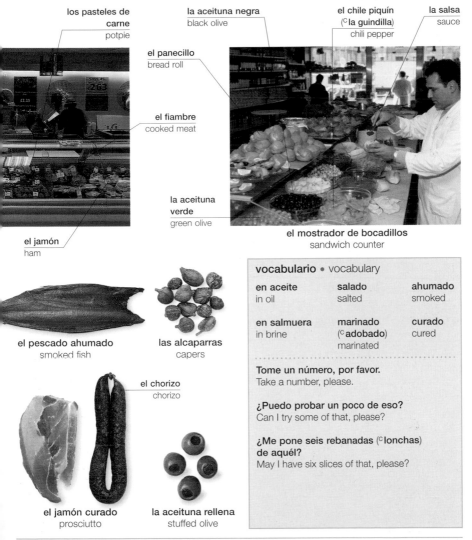

los pasteles de carne
potpie

la aceituna negra
black olive

el chile piquín
(ᶜla guindilla)
chili pepper

la salsa
sauce

el panecillo
bread roll

el fiambre
cooked meat

la aceituna verde
green olive

el jamón
ham

el mostrador de bocadillos
sandwich counter

el pescado ahumado
smoked fish

las alcaparras
capers

el chorizo
chorizo

el jamón curado
prosciutto

la aceituna rellena
stuffed olive

vocabulario • vocabulary

en aceite in oil	salado salted	ahumado smoked
en salmuera in brine	marinado (ᶜadobado) marinated	curado cured

Tome un número, por favor.
Take a number, please.

¿Puedo probar un poco de eso?
Can I try some of that, please?

¿Me pone seis rebanadas (ᶜlonchas) de aquél?
May I have six slices of that, please?

las bebidas • drinks

el agua • water

el agua embotellada
bottled water

con gas
sparkling

sin gas
still

el agua de la llave
(ᶜdel grifo)
tap water

la tónica
tonic water

la soda
soda water

el agua mineral
mineral water

las bebidas calientes • hot drinks

la bolsita de té
teabag

el té en hoja
loose-leaf tea

el té
tea

los granos
beans

el café molido
ground coffee

el café
coffee

el chocolate
caliente
hot chocolate

la bebida
malteada
malted drink

los refrescos • soft drinks

el popote
(ᶜla pajita)
straw

el jugo de jitomate
(ᶜel zumo de tomate)
tomato juice

el jugo (ᶜel
zumo) de uva
grape juice

la limonada
lemonade

la naranjada
orangeade

la cola
cola

las bebidas alcohólicas • alcoholic drinks

la ginebra
gin

la lata
can

la cerveza
beer

la sidra
hard cider

la cerveza amarga
bitter

la cerveza negra
stout

el vodka
vodka

el whisky
whiskey

el ron
rum

el brandy (ᶜel coñac)
brandy

el oporto
port

seco
dry

el vino de jerez
sherry

el campari
Campari

rosado
rosé

blanco
white

tinto
red

el licor
liqueur

el tequila
tequila

el champán
champagne

el vino
wine

comer fuera
eating out

la cafetería • café

la sombrilla
umbrella

el toldo
awning

la carta
menu

la terraza
patio café

el mesero
(ᶜel camarero)
server

la máquina de café
coffee machine

la mesa
table

la cafetería con mesas fuera | sidewalk café

el bar | snack bar

el café • coffee

el café con leche
coffee with milk

el café solo
black coffee

la cocoa (ᶜel cacao en polvo)
cocoa powder

la espuma
froth

el café de cafetera eléctrica
filter coffee

el expreso (ᶜel café solo)
espresso

el cappuccino
cappuccino

el café con hielo
iced coffee

el té • tea

el té de hierbas
(^C la infusión)
herbal tea

la manzanilla
chamomile tea

el té verde
green tea

el té con leche
tea with milk

el té negro
black tea

el té con limón
tea with lemon

la menta poleo
mint tea

el té con hielo
iced tea

los jugos y las malteadas (^C los zumos y los batidos) • juices and milkshakes

la malteada de chocolate
(^C el batido de chocolate)
chocolate milkshake

la malteada de fresa (^C el batido de fresa)
strawberry milkshake

el jugo de naranja
orange juice

el jugo de manzana (^C el zumo de manzana)
apple juice

el jugo de piña
pineapple juice

el jugo de jitomate (^C el zumo de tomate)
tomato juice

la malteada de café (^C el batido de café)
coffee milkshake

la comida • food

el pan integral
whole-wheat bread

la bola
scoop

el sandwich tostado
toasted sandwich

la ensalada
salad

el helado
ice cream

el pan dulce (^C el pastel)
pastry

el bar • bar

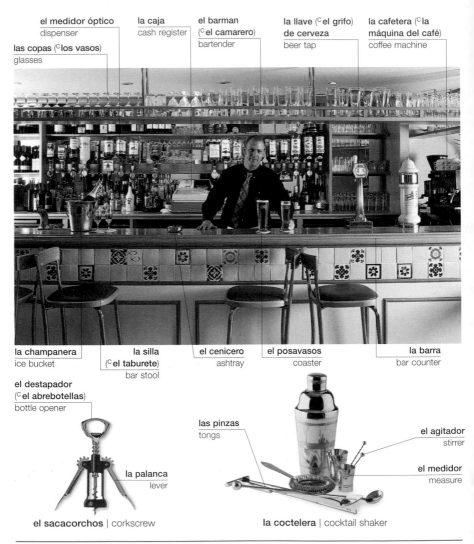

el medidor óptico
dispenser

las copas (C los vasos)
glasses

la caja
cash register

el barman
(C el camarero)
bartender

la llave (C el grifo)
de cerveza
beer tap

la cafetera (C la
máquina del café)
coffee machine

la champanera
ice bucket

la silla
(C el taburete)
bar stool

el cenicero
ashtray

el posavasos
coaster

la barra
bar counter

el destapador
(C el abrebotellas)
bottle opener

las pinzas
tongs

el agitador
stirrer

el medidor
measure

la palanca
lever

el sacacorchos | corkscrew

la coctelera | cocktail shaker

la jarra
pitcher

el cubito de hielo
ice cube

el gin tonic
gin and tonic

el whiskey escocés con agua
scotch and water

cuba libre
(ᶜcuba libre/ron cola)
rum and cola

el desarmador
(ᶜel vodka con naranja)
screwdriver

el martini
martini

el cóctel
cocktail

el vino
wine

la cerveza | beer

doble
double

sencillo
single

con hielo y limón
ice and lemon

un trago
shot

la medida
measure

sin hielo
without ice

con hielo
with ice

la botana (ᶜ los aperitivos) • bar snacks

las nueces de la India
(ᶜlos anacardos)
cashews

las almendras
almonds

los cacahuetes
peanuts

las papas (ᶜlas patatas) fritas
potato chips

los frutos secos | nuts

las aceitunas | olives

el restaurante • restaurant

el cubierto
table setting

el ayudante
del chef
sous chef

el chef
chef

la copa
glass

la charola
(^C la bandeja)
tray

la cocina
kitchen

el mesero (^C el camarero)
server

---

vocabulario • vocabulary

la lista de vinos wine list	**a la carta** à la carte	**el precio** price	**la propina** tip	**el bufet** buffet	**el cliente** customer
el menú de la comida lunch menu	**el carrito de los postres** dessert cart	**la cuenta** check	**servicio incluido** service charge included	**el bar** bar	**la pimienta** pepper
el menú de la cena dinner menu	**los platillos (^Clos platos) del día** specials	**el recibo** receipt	**servicio no incluido** service charge not included	**la sal** salt	

---

español • english

la carta
menu

el menú para niños
child's meal

ordenar (^c**pedir**)
order (v)

pagar
pay (v)

los platos • courses

el aperitivo
apéritif

la entrada
(^c**el entrante**)
appetizer

la sopa
soup

el plato principal
entrée

el acompañamiento
side order

el postre | dessert

el café | coffee

Una mesa para dos, por favor.
A table for two, please.

¿Podría ver la carta/lista de vinos, por favor?
Can I see the menu/wine list, please?

¿Hay menú del día?
Is there a fixed-price menu?

¿Tiene platos vegetarianos?
Do you have any vegetarian dishes?

¿Me podría traer la cuenta/un recibo?
Could I have the check/a receipt, please?

¿Podemos pagar por separado?
Can we pay separately?

¿Dónde están los baños (^clos servicios), por favor?
Where is the restroom, please?

la comida rápida • fast food

el popote (^Cla pajita)
straw

la hamburguesa
burger

el refresco
soft drink

las papas fritas
(^Clas patatas fritas)
French fries

la servilleta de papel
paper napkin

la charola
(^Cla bandeja)
tray

la hamburguesa con papas fritas (^Cla hamburguesa con patatas fritas) | burger meal

la pizza
pizza

la lista de precios
price list

el refresco en lata
(^Cla lata de bebida)
canned drink

la entrega a domicilio
home delivery

el puesto callejero
street vendor

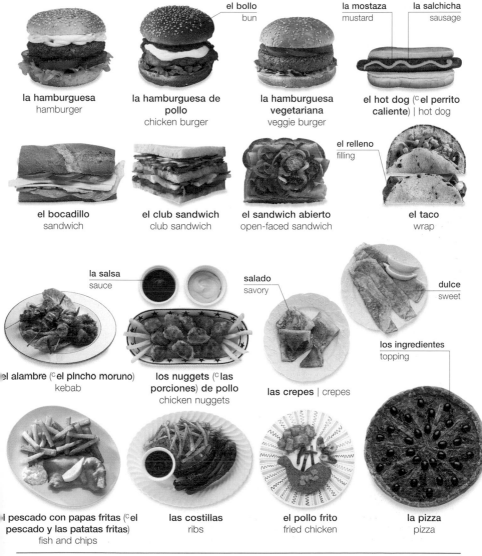

el bollo
bun

la mostaza
mustard

la salchicha
sausage

la hamburguesa
hamburger

la hamburguesa de pollo
chicken burger

la hamburguesa vegetariana
veggie burger

el hot dog (ᶜel perrito caliente) | hot dog

el relleno
filling

el bocadillo
sandwich

el club sandwich
club sandwich

el sandwich abierto
open-faced sandwich

el taco
wrap

la salsa
sauce

salado
savory

dulce
sweet

los ingredientes
topping

el alambre (ᶜel pincho moruno)
kebab

los nuggets (ᶜlas porciones) de pollo
chicken nuggets

las crepes | crepes

el pescado con papas fritas (ᶜel pescado y las patatas fritas)
fish and chips

las costillas
ribs

el pollo frito
fried chicken

la pizza
pizza

el desayuno • breakfast

la leche | milk

los **cereales** | cereal

la **mermelada** | jam

la **fruta seca** (^C**desecada**) | dried fruit

el **jamón** | ham

el **queso** | cheese

la **galleta de centeno** | crispbread

el buffet de desayuno | breakfast buffet

la mermelada de naranja | marmalade

el paté | pâté

la mantequilla | butter

el **jugo** (^C**el zumo**) **de frutas** | fruit juice

el **café** | coffee

el **chocolate caliente** (^C**el cacao**) | hot chocolate

el **croissant** | croissant

el **té** | tea

la mesa del desayuno | breakfast table

las bebidas | drinks

el jitomate
(^{C}el tomate)
tomato

la morcilla
black pudding

el pan tostado
toast

la salchicha
sausage

el huevo
estrellado (^{C}frito)
fried egg

el tocino
(^{C}el bacon)
bacon

el desayuno inglés
English breakfast

el brioche
brioche

el pan
bread

la yema
yolk

**los arenques
ahumados**
kippers

el pan francés
(^{C}la torrija)
French toast

el huevo tibio
(^{C}pasado por agua)
soft-boiled egg

los huevos revueltos
scrambled eggs

la crema (^{C}la nata)
whipped cream

el yogurt de frutas
fruit yogurt

los crepes
crepes

los waffles (^{C}los gofres)
waffles

la avena (^{C}las
gachas de avena)
oatmeal

la fruta fresca
fresh fruit

la comida principal • dinner

la sopa | soup

el caldo | broth

el guiso | stew

el curry | curry

el asado
roast

la empanada (ᶜel pastel)
potpie

el soufflé
soufflé

la brocheta (ᶜel pincho)
kebab

las albóndigas
meatballs

el omelette (ᶜla tortilla)
omelet

los fideos
noodles

el fritura | stir-fry

la pasta | pasta

el arroz
rice

la ensalada mixta
tossed salad

la ensalada verde
green salad

el aderezo (ᶜel aliño)
dressing

las técnicas • techniques

relleno | stuffed

en salsa | in sauce

a la plancha | grilled

adobado | marinated

escalfado | poached

hecho puré | mashed

al horno (ᶜ**cocido en el horno**) | baked

frito con poco aceite
pan-fried

frito
fried

en vinagre
pickled

ahumado
smoked

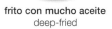
frito con mucho aceite
deep-fried

en almíbar
in syrup

sazonado (ᶜ**aliñado**)
dressed

al vapor
steamed

curado
cured

el estudio
study

el colegio • school

el pizarrón (^C**la pizarrón blanco**)
whiteboard

la maestra (^C**la profesora**)
teacher

la mochila (^C**la cartera**)
schoolbag

el alumno
student

el pupitre
desk

el aula | classroom

la colegiala
schoolgirl

el colegial
schoolboy

---

vocabulario • vocabulary

la historia history	**el arte** art	**la física** physics
la literatura literature	**la música** music	**la química** chemistry
los idiomas languages	**la ciencia** science	**la biología** biology
la geografía geography	**las matemáticas** math	**la educación física** physical education

las actividades • activities

leer | read (v)

escribir | write (v)

deletrear
spell (v)

dibujar
draw (v)

la punta
nib

el color
(C el lápiz de colores)
colored pencil

el
sacapuntas
pencil
sharpener

el proyector digital
digital projector

la pluma
(C el bolígrafo)
pen

el lápiz
pencil

el cuaderno
notebook

la goma
eraser

el libro de texto | textbook

el estuche
pencil case

la regla
ruler

preguntar
question (v)

contestar
answer (v)

discutir
discuss (v)

aprender
learn (v)

vocabulario • vocabulary

el director
principal

la respuesta
answer

el diccionario
dictionary

la lección
lesson

la redacción
essay

la enciclopedia
encyclopedia

la question
(C la pregunta)
question

la tarea
(C los deberes)
homework

la calificación
(C la nota)
grade

tomar
apuntes
take notes (v)

el examen
test

el año
(C el curso)
year

las matemáticas • math

las formas • shapes

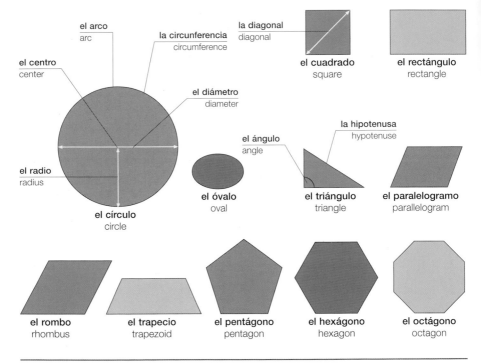

el arco
arc

la circunferencia
circumference

la diagonal
diagonal

el cuadrado
square

el rectángulo
rectangle

el centro
center

el diámetro
diameter

el radio
radius

el ángulo
angle

la hipotenusa
hypotenuse

el círculo
circle

el óvalo
oval

el triángulo
triangle

el paralelogramo
parallelogram

el rombo
rhombus

el trapecio
trapezoid

el pentágono
pentagon

el hexágono
hexagon

el octágono
octagon

los cuerpos geométricos • solids

la base
base

el lado
side

el ápice
apex

el cono
cone

el cilindro
cylinder

el cubo
cube

la pirámide
pyramid

la esfera
sphere

las líneas • lines

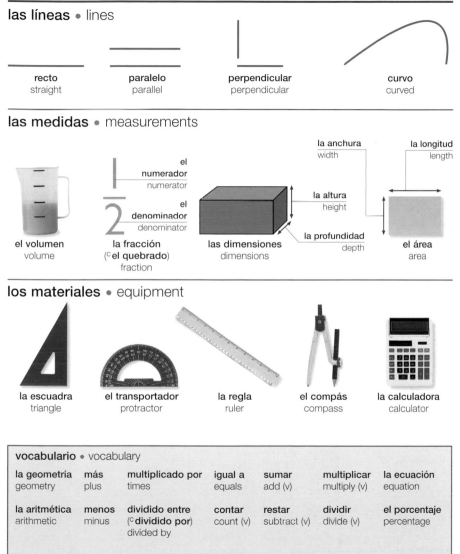

recto
straight

paralelo
parallel

perpendicular
perpendicular

curvo
curved

las medidas • measurements

el volumen
volume

el
numerador
numerator

el
denominador
denominator

la fracción
(ᶜ **el quebrado**)
fraction

las dimensiones
dimensions

la anchura
width

la longitud
length

la altura
height

la profundidad
depth

el área
area

los materiales • equipment

la escuadra
triangle

el transportador
protractor

la regla
ruler

el compás
compass

la calculadora
calculator

---

vocabulario • vocabulary

la geometría geometry	**más** plus	**multiplicado por** times	**igual a** equals	**sumar** add (v)	**multiplicar** multiply (v)	**la ecuación** equation
la aritmética arithmetic	**menos** minus	**dividido entre** (ᶜ **dividido por**) divided by	**contar** count (v)	**restar** subtract (v)	**dividir** divide (v)	**el porcentaje** percentage

---

las ciencias • science

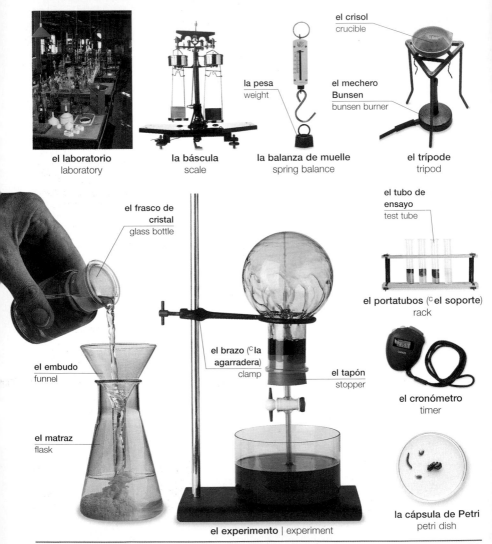

el laboratorio
laboratory

la báscula
scale

la pesa
weight

la balanza de muelle
spring balance

el crisol
crucible

el mechero Bunsen
bunsen burner

el trípode
tripod

el frasco de cristal
glass bottle

el tubo de ensayo
test tube

el portatubos (ᶜel soporte)
rack

el embudo
funnel

el brazo (ᶜla agarradera)
clamp

el tapón
stopper

el cronómetro
timer

el matraz
flask

la cápsula de Petri
petri dish

el experimento | experiment

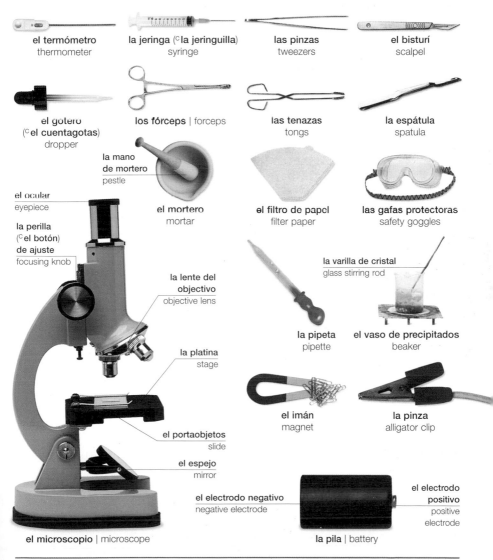

el termómetro
thermometer

la jeringa (ᶜ**la jeringuilla**)
syringe

las pinzas
tweezers

el bisturí
scalpel

el gotero
(ᶜ**el cuentagotas**)
dropper

los fórceps | forceps

las tenazas
tongs

la espátula
spatula

la mano de mortero
pestle

el mortero
mortar

el filtro de papel
filter paper

las gafas protectoras
safety goggles

el ocular
eyepiece

la perilla
(ᶜ**el botón**)
de ajuste
focusing knob

la lente del objectivo
objective lens

la platina
stage

el portaobjetos
slide

el espejo
mirror

la varilla de cristal
glass stirring rod

la pipeta
pipette

el vaso de precipitados
beaker

el imán
magnet

la pinza
alligator clip

el electrodo negativo
negative electrode

el electrodo positivo
positive electrode

el microscopio | microscope

la pila | battery

la enseñanza superior • college

la secretaría
admissions
office

el comedor
(^C el refectorio)
cafeteria

el centro de salud
health center

el campo
de deportes
playing field

la residencia
estudiantil
(^C el colegio
mayor)
residence hall

el campus | campus

---

vocabulario • vocabulary		
el préstamo loan	**la información** help desk	**renovar** renew (v)
reservar reserve (v)	**coger prestado** borrow (v)	**el libro** book
la lista de lecturas reading list	**la sala de lecturas** reading room	**el título** title
la fecha de devolución due date	**la credencial** (^C**la tarjeta de la biblioteca**) library card	**el pasillo** aisle

la bibliotecaria
librarian

el mostrador de
préstamos
circulation desk

el librero (^C la
estantería)
bookshelf

el periódico
periodical

la revista
journal

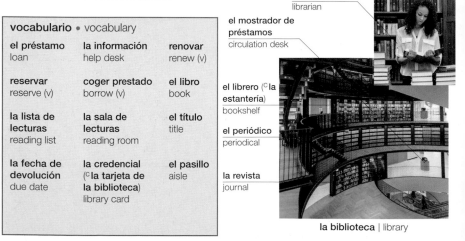

la biblioteca | library

el estudiante
undergraduate

el profesor
professor

la licenciada
graduate

la toga
gown

el auditorio (ᶜel anfiteatro)
lecture hall

la ceremonia de graduación
graduation ceremony

las escuelas • schools

la modelo
model

la escuela de Bellas Artes
art school

el conservatorio
music school

la academia de danza
dance school

vocabulario • vocabulary

la beca scholarship	**la investigación** research	**la tesina** dissertation	**la medicina** medicine	**la sciencas políticas** political science
el diploma diploma	**el doctorado** doctorate	**el departamento** department	**la zoología** zoology	**la literatura** literature
la carrera degree	**la tesis** thesis	**el derecho** law	**la física** physics	**la historia del arte** art history
posgrado postgraduate	**la maestría** (ᶜel máster) master's	**la ingeniería** engineering	**la filosofía** philosophy	**las ciencias económicas** economics

el trabajo
work

la oficina 1 • office 1

el portaplumas
(^C **el portabolígrafos**)
desktop organizer

la pantalla
monitor

la bandeja de entrada
in-tray

el ordenador portátil
laptop

el cuaderno
notebook

la bandeja de salida
out-tray

el cajón
drawer

el escritorio
desk

la silla giratoria
swivel chair

el bote de basura
(^C **la papelera**)
wastebasket

el archivero
(^C **el archivador**)
filing cabinet

---

el equipo de oficina • office equipment

la bandeja para el papel
paper tray

la impresora | printer

destructora de papel
shredder

vocabulario • vocabulary	
imprimir print (v)	**ampliar** enlarge (v)
fotocopiar copy (v)	**reducir** reduce (v)

Necesito sacar (^C **hacer**) **unas copias.**
I need to make some copies.

los materiales de oficina • office supplies

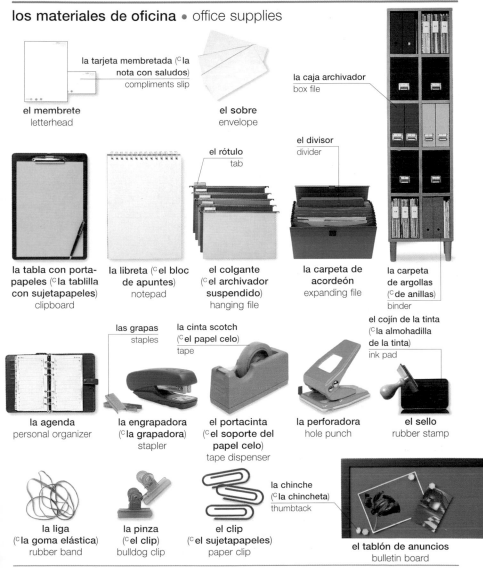

el membrete
letterhead

la tarjeta membretada (^{C}**la nota con saludos**)
compliments slip

el sobre
envelope

la caja archivador
box file

el rótulo
tab

el divisor
divider

la tabla con porta-papeles (^{C}**la tablilla con sujetapapeles**)
clipboard

la libreta (^{C}**el bloc de apuntes**)
notepad

el colgante (^{C}**el archivador suspendido**)
hanging file

la carpeta de acordeón
expanding file

la carpeta de argollas (^{C}**de anillas**)
binder

la agenda
personal organizer

las grapas
staples

la cinta scotch (^{C}**el papel celo**)
tape

la engrapadora (^{C}**la grapadora**)
stapler

el portacinta (^{C}**el soporte del papel celo**)
tape dispenser

la perforadora
hole punch

el cojín de la tinta (^{C}**la almohadilla de la tinta**)
ink pad

el sello
rubber stamp

la liga (^{C}**la goma elástica**)
rubber band

la pinza (^{C}**el clip**)
bulldog clip

el clip (^{C}**el sujetapapeles**)
paper clip

la chinche (^{C}**la chincheta**)
thumbtack

el tablón de anuncios
bulletin board

la oficina 2 • office 2

el pizarrón
(^C**el rotafolio**)
flip chart

el caballete
easel

la minuta
(^C **el acta**)
minutes

el gerente
manager

la propuesta
proposal

el reporte
(^C**el informe**)
report

el ejecutivo
executive

la junta (^Cla reunión) | meeting

---

vocabulario • vocabulary

el orden del día
agenda

asistir
attend (v)

la sala de juntas (^C**reuniones**)
meeting room

presidir
chair (v)

¿A qué hora es la junta (^Cla reunión)?
What time is the meeting?

¿Cuál es su horario de oficina?
What are your office hours?

la oradora
speaker

la presentación | presentation

---

los negocios • business

el hombre de negocios
businessman

la mujer de negocios
businesswoman

la comida de negocios
business lunch

el viaje de negocios
business trip

la cita
appointment

el director general
CEO

la clienta
client

la agenda | day planner

el trato
business deal

vocabulario • vocabulary

la empresa company	el personal staff	el departamento de ventas sales department	el departamento legal legal department
la oficina central head office	la nómina payroll	el departamento de contabilidad accounting department	el departamento de atención al cliente customer service department
la sucursal regional office	el sueldo salary	el departamento de márketing marketing department	el departamento de recursos humanos human resources department

la computadora (^Cel ordenador) • computer

la impresora
printer

la pantalla
screen

el escáner
scanner

el ordenador portátil
laptop

la tecla
key

el teclado
keyboard

el ratón
mouse

la bocina (^Cel altavoz)
speaker

el hardware
hardware

la llave de memoria
memory stick

el disco duro externo
external hard drive

vocabulario • vocabulary		
la memoria memory	**el software** software	**el servidor** server
el RAM RAM	**la aplicación** application	**el puerto** port
los bytes bytes	**el programa** program	**el precesador** processor
el sistema system	**la red** network	**el cable de alimentación** power cord

la tablet
tablet

el teléfono inteligente
smartphone

el escritorio • desktop

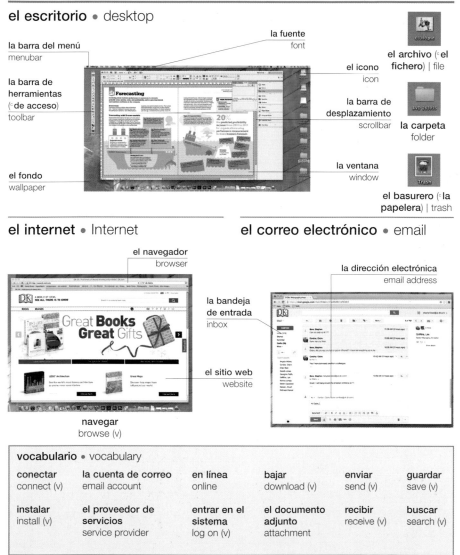

la barra del menú
menubar

la fuente
font

el icono
icon

el archivo (ᵒ el **fichero**) | file

la barra de herramientas
(ᵒ **de acceso**)
toolbar

la barra de desplazamiento
scrollbar

la carpeta
folder

el fondo
wallpaper

la ventana
window

el basurero (ᵒ **la papelera**) | trash

el internet • Internet

el navegador
browser

navegar
browse (v)

el correo electrónico • email

la dirección electrónica
email address

la bandeja de entrada
inbox

el sitio web
website

vocabulario • vocabulary

conectar connect (v)	**la cuenta de correo** email account	**en línea** online	**bajar** download (v)	**enviar** send (v)	**guardar** save (v)
instalar install (v)	**el proveedor de servicios** service provider	**entrar en el sistema** log on (v)	**el documento adjunto** attachment	**recibir** receive (v)	**buscar** search (v)

los medios de comunicación • media

el estudio de televisión • television studio

el plató
set

el presentador
host

el reflector (^Cel foco)
light

la cámara
camera

la grúa de la cámara
camera crane

el camarógrafo
(^Cel cámara)
cameraman

vocabulario • vocabulary

el canal channel	el documental documentary	la prensa press	la telenovela soap opera	el concurso game show	en directo live
la programación programming	el noticiario news	la serie televisiva television series	transmitir (^Cemitir) broadcast (v)	las caricaturas (^Clos dibujos animados) cartoon	pregrabado (^Cen diferido) prerecorded

el entrevistador
interviewer

la reportera
reporter

el teleprompter
(^C **el autocue**)
teleprompter

la presentadora de las noticias
anchor

los actores
actors

el micrófono de aire
(^C **la jirafa**) | sound boom

la pizarra (^C **la claqueta**)
clapper board

el plató de rodaje
movie set

la radio • radio

el técnico de sonido
sound technician

la consola
(^C **la mesa de mezclas**)
mixing desk

el micrófono
microphone

el estudio de grabación | recording studio

vocabulario • vocabulary	
la estación de radio radio station	**la onda media** medium wave
el DJ (^C **el pinchadiscos**) DJ	**la frecuencia** frequency
la transmisión (^C **la emisión**) broadcast	**el volumen** volume
la longitud de onda wavelength	**sintonizar** tune (v)
la onda larga long wave	**analógico** analog
la onda corta short wave	**digital** digital

el derecho • law

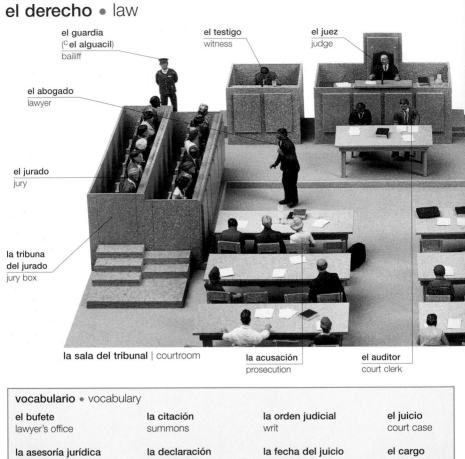

el guardia
(ᶜel alguacil)
bailiff

el testigo
witness

el juez
judge

el abogado
lawyer

el jurado
jury

la tribuna
del jurado
jury box

la sala del tribunal | courtroom

la acusación
prosecution

el auditor
court clerk

---

vocabulario • vocabulary

el bufete lawyer's office	**la citación** summons	**la orden judicial** writ	**el juicio** court case
la asesoría jurídica legal advice	**la declaración** statement	**la fecha del juicio** court date	**el cargo** charge
el cliente client	**la orden judicial** warrant	**la súplica** plea	**el acusado** accused

---

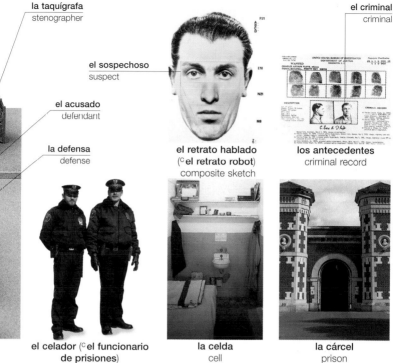

la taquígrafa
stenographer

el sospechoso
suspect

el acusado
defendant

la defensa
defense

el criminal
criminal

el retrato hablado
(ᶜel retrato robot)
composite sketch

los antecedentes
criminal record

el celador (ᶜel funcionario
de prisiones)
prison guard

la celda
cell

la cárcel
prison

vocabulario • vocabulary

lel veredicto verdict	**absuelto** acquitted	**la fianza** bail	**Quiero ver a un abogado.** I want to see a lawyer.
inocente innocent	**la sentencia** sentence	**la apelación** appeal	**¿Dónde está el juzgado?** Where is the courthouse?
culpable guilty	**la evidencia** (ᶜ**la prueba**) evidence	**la libertad condicional** parole	**¿Puedo pagar la fianza?** Can I post bail?

la granja 1 • farm 1

las tierras de labranza
farmland

el corral
farmyard

el cobertizo
outbuilding

la casa de labranza
farmhouse

el campo
field

el granjero
farmer

el granero
barn

el huerto
vegetable garden

el seto
hedge

la puerta
gate

la cerca
fence

el pasto
pasture

el ganado
livestock

el cultivador
cultivator

el tractor | tractor

la cosechadora | combine

los tipos de granja • types of farms

la cosecha
crop

la granja de tierras cultivables
crop farm

la vaquería
dairy farm

el rebaño
flock

la granja de ganado ovino
sheep farm

la granja avícola
poultry farm

la granja de ganado porcino
pig farm

el criadero de peces
(ᶜ**la piscifactoría**)
fish farm

la granja de frutales
fruit farm

la viña (ᶜla vid)
vine

el viñedo
vineyard

las actividades • actions

el surco
furrow

arar
plow (v)

sembrar
sow (v)

ordeñar
milk (v)

alimentar (ᶜdar de comer)
feed (v)

regar | water (v)

recolectar | harvest (v)

vocabulario • vocabulary

el herbicida herbicide	**la manada** herd	**el comedero** trough
el pesticida pesticide	**el silo** silo	**plantar** plant (v)

la granja 2 • farm 2

los cultivos (ᶜlas cosechas) • crops

el trigo
wheat

el maíz
corn

la cebada
barley

la colza
rapeseed

el girasol
sunflower

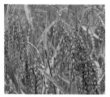
la paca
(ᶜla bala)
bale

el heno
hay

la alfalfa
alfalfa

el tabaco
tobacco

el arroz
rice

el té
tea

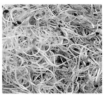
el café
coffee

el lino
flax

la caña de azúcar
sugarcane

el algodón
cotton

el espantapájaros
scarecrow

el ganado • livestock

el chanchito
(ᵉel lechón)
piglet

el puerco (ᵉel cerdo)
pig

el ternero
calf

la vaca
cow

el toro
bull

la oveja
sheep

el cabrito
kid

el cordero
lamb

la cabra
goat

el potro
foal

el caballo
horse

el burro
donkey

el pollito
(ᵉel polluelo)
chick

la gallina
chicken

el gallo
rooster

el guajolote (ᵉel pavo)
turkey

el patito
duckling

el pato
duck

el establo
stable

el redil
pen

el gallinero
chicken coop

el chiquero (ᵉla pocilga)
pigsty

la construcción • construction

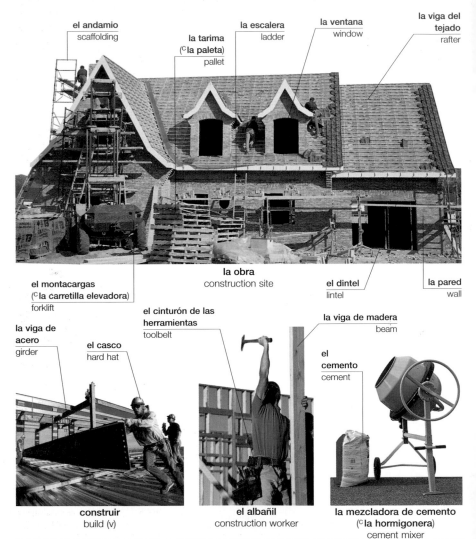

el andamio
scaffolding

la tarima
(^Cla paleta)
pallet

la escalera
ladder

la ventana
window

la viga del
tejado
rafter

el montacargas
(^Cla carretilla elevadora)
forklift

la obra
construction site

el dintel
lintel

la pared
wall

la viga de
acero
girder

el casco
hard hat

el cinturón de las
herramientas
toolbelt

la viga de madera
beam

el
cemento
cement

construir
build (v)

el albañil
construction worker

la mezcladora de cemento
(^Cla hormigonera)
cement mixer

los materiales • materials

el ladrillo
brick

la madera
lumber

la teja
roof tile

bloque de hormigón
cinder block

las herramientas • tools

la argamasa
mortar

la paleta
trowel

el nivel
level

el mango
handle

el mazo
sledgehammer

el zapapico
(ᶜ**el pico**)
pickax

la pala
shovel

la maquinaria • machinery

la aplanadora
(ᶜ**la apisonadora**)
road roller

el camión de volteo
(ᶜ**el camión volquete**)
dump truck

el soporte
support

el gancho
hook

la grúa | crane

las obras viales (ᶜ**las obras**) • roadwork

el asfalto
asphalt

el cono
cone

el martillo
neumático
jackhammer

el revestimiento
resurfacing

la pala mecánica
(ᶜ**la excavadora mecánica**)
excavator

las profesiones 1 • occupations 1

el carpintero
carpenter

el electricista
electrician

el plomero (^Cel fontanero)
plumber

el albañil
construction worker

el jardinero
gardener

la
aspiradora
vacuum
cleaner

el empleado de la
limpieza
cleaner

el mecánico
mechanic

el carnicero
butcher

el estilista
(^C el peluquero)
hairdresser

la pescadera
fish seller

el frutero
produce seller

la florista
florist

el peluquero
(^C el barbero)
barber

el joyero
jeweler

la vendedora
(^C la dependienta)
salesperson

la agente inmobiliaria
realtor

el optometrista
(^C **el óptico**) | optometrist

la mascarilla
mask
la dentista
dentist

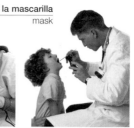
el médico
doctor

la farmacéutica
pharmacist

la enfermera
nurse

la veterinaria
veterinarian

el agricultor
farmer

el pescador
fisherman

la metralleta
machine gun

la placa de
identificación
badge

el uniforme
uniform

**el guardia de
seguridad**
security guard

el marino
sailor

el soldado
soldier

el policía
police officer

el bombero
firefighter

las profesiones 2 • occupations 2

la abogada
lawyer

el contador (ᶜ el contable)
accountant

la maqueta
model

el arquitecto
architect

la científica
scientist

la maestra (ᶜ la profesora)
teacher

el bibliotecario
librarian

la recepcionista
receptionist

la cartera
mailbag

el cartero
mail carrier

el conductor de atobús
bus driver

el chófer
(ᶜ el camionero)
truck driver

el taxista
taxi driver

el piloto
pilot

la sobrecargo
(ᶜ la azafata)
flight attendant

el gorro de
cocinero
chef's hat

el cocinero
chef

la agente de viajes
travel agent

190

el músico
musician

el tutú
tutu

la bailarina
dancer

la actriz
actress

la cantante
singer

la mesera
(ᶜ la camarera)
waitress

el barman
(ᶜ el camarero)
bartender

el deportista
sportsman

el escultor
sculptor

la pintora
painter

el fotógrafo
photographer

la presentadora
anchor

las notas
notes

el periodista
journalist

la redactora
editor

el diseñador
designer

la modista
seamstress

el sastre
tailor

el transporte
transportation

las carreteras • roads

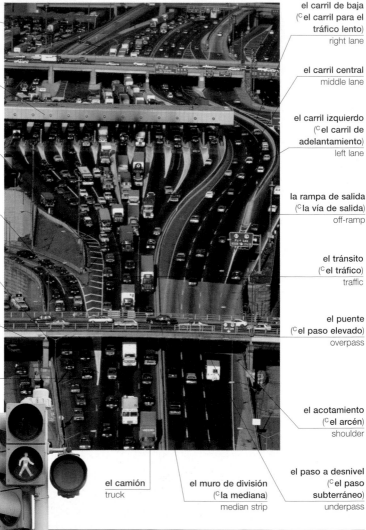

la autopista
freeway

la caseta de
cobro (^C de peaje)
toll booth

las señales de piso
(^C las señales
horizontales)
road markings

la entrada
(^C la vía de acceso)
on-ramp

la calle de
sentido único
one-way

la línea divisoria
divider

el crucero
(^C el cruce)
interchange

el semáforo
traffic light

el camión
truck

el carril de baja
(^C el carril para el
tráfico lento)
right lane

el carril central
middle lane

el carril izquierdo
(^C el carril de
adelantamiento)
left lane

la rampa de salida
(^C la vía de salida)
off-ramp

el tránsito
(^C el tráfico)
traffic

el puente
(^C el paso elevado)
overpass

el acotamiento
(^C el arcén)
shoulder

el muro de división
(^C la mediana)
median strip

el paso a desnivel
(^C el paso
subterráneo)
underpass

el teléfono de emergencia
emergency phone

el estacionamiento
(ᶜel aparcamiento)
para minusválidos
disabled parking

el paso de peatones
crosswalk

el tráfico (ᶜel atasco de tráfico)
traffic jam

el navegador por satélite
satnav

el parquímetro
parking meter

el policía vial
(ᶜel policía de tráfico)
traffic policeman

vocabulario • vocabulary

la desviación (ᶜel desvío) detour	**manejar** (ᶜconducir) drive (v)	**remolcar** tow away (v)
estacionar (ᶜaparcar) park (v)	**rebasar** (ᶜadelantar) pass (v)	**la autovía** divided highway
la glorieta roundabout	**las obras** roadwork	**¿Es ésta la carretera hacia...?** Is this the road to...?
meter reversa (ᶜdar marcha atrás) reverse (v)	**el muro de contención** (ᶜla barrera de seguridad) guardrail	**¿Dónde me puedo estacionar** (ᶜaparcar)**?** Where can I park?

las señales de tránsito • road signs

prohibido el paso
do not enter

el límite de velocidad
speed limit

peligro
hazard

prohibido parar
no stopping

no dar vuelta (ᶜno torcer) **a la derecha**
no right turn

el autobús • bus

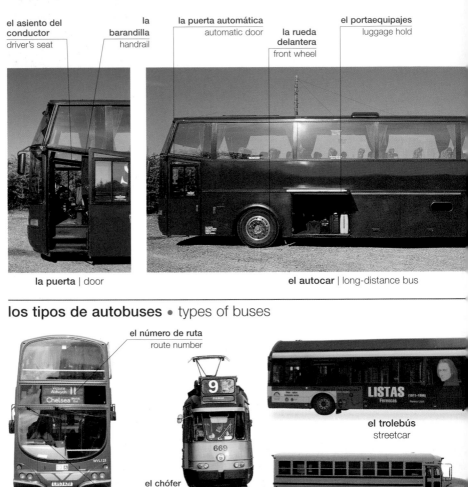

el asiento del conductor
driver's seat

la barandilla
handrail

la puerta automática
automatic door

la rueda delantera
front wheel

el portaequipajes
luggage hold

la puerta | door

el autocar | long-distance bus

los tipos de autobuses • types of buses

el número de ruta
route number

el chófer
(ᶜel conductor)
driver

el autobús de dos pisos
double-decker bus

el tranvía
tram

el trolebús
streetcar

el autobús escolar | school bus

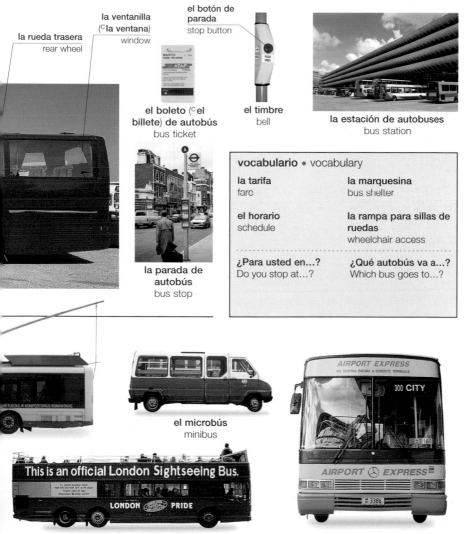

la rueda trasera
rear wheel

la ventanilla
(ᶜ **la ventana**)
window

el botón de parada
stop button

el boleto (ᶜ**el billete) de autobús**
bus ticket

el timbre
bell

la estación de autobuses
bus station

la parada de autobús
bus stop

vocabulario • vocabulary

la tarifa fare	**la marquesina** bus shelter
el horario schedule	**la rampa para sillas de ruedas** wheelchair access
¿Para usted en…? Do you stop at…?	**¿Qué autobús va a…?** Which bus goes to…?

el microbús
minibus

el autobús turístico | tour bus

el autobús directo (ᶜ**de enlace) | shuttle bus**

el carro (^Cel coche) 1 • car 1

el exterior • exterior

el espejo lateral
(^Cel retrovisor
exterior)
side mirror

el parabrisas
windshield

el espejo
retrovisor
rearview mirror

el limpiaparabrisas
windshield wiper

la puerta
door

la cajuela
(^Cel
maletero)
trunk

el cofre
(^Cel capó)
hood

la direccional
(^Cel intermitente)
turn signal

la defensa (^Cel
parachoques)
bumper

la matrícula
license plate

el faro
headlight

la rueda
wheel

la llanta (^Cel
neumático)
tire

el equipaje
luggage

la baca
roof rack

la puerta abatible
(^Cla puerta del maletero)
tailgate

el cinturón de
seguridad
seat belt

la silla para niños
car seat

los modelos • types

el coche eléctrico
electric car

**el carro (ᶜel coche)
de cinco puertas**
hatchback

el carro familiar
(ᶜel turismo)
sedan

la camioneta
(ᶜel coche ranchera)
station wagon

el convertible
(ᶜel coche descapotable)
convertible

el coche deportivo
sports car

la minivan
(ᶜel monovolumen)
minivan

la doble tracción
(ᶜel todoterreno)
four-wheel drive

el auto (ᶜel coche) de época
vintage

la limousina
limousine

la gasolinera • gas station

la bomba
(ᶜel surtidor)
gas pump

el precio
price

VALERO
cornerstore
UNLEAD 2.5 9⁹
DIESEL 2.4 9⁹
TOUCHLESS
CAR WASH
SUBWAY

la zona de abastecimiento
forecourt

vocabulario • vocabulary

el aceite oil	**el diesel** diesel	**el anticongelante** antifreeze
la gasolina gasoline	**con plomo** leaded	**el auto-lavado** (ᶜel lavadero de coches) car wash
sin plomo unleaded	**el taller** garage	**el líquido limpiaparabrisas** windshield washer fluid

Llénelo (ᶜLleno), por favor.
Fill it up, please.

el carro (^Cel coche) 2 • car 2

el interior • interior

el asiento trasero	el reposabrazos	el reposacabezas	el seguro (^Cel pestillo)	la manija (^Cel tirador)
backseat	armrest	headrest	door lock	handle

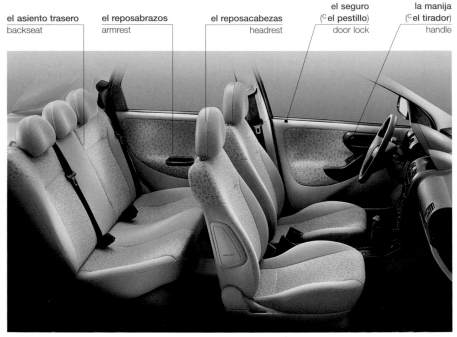

---

vocabulario • vocabulary

dos puertas	de cuatro	automático	el freno	el acelerador
two-door	**puertas**	automatic	brake	accelerator
	four-door			

de tres		el	el	el aire
puertas	**manual**	**encendido**	**embrague**	**acondicionado**
hatchback	manual	ignition	clutch	air-conditioning

¿Me puede decir cómo se va a...?	**¿Dónde hay un estacionamiento** (^C**parking)?**	**¿Se puede estacionar** (^C**aparcar) aquí?**
Can you tell me the way to...?	Where is the parking lot?	Can I park here?

---

los controles • controls

| el volante steering wheel | el claxon (^Cla bocina) horn | el tablero (^Cel salpicadero) dashboard | las luces de emergencia hazard lights | la navegación por satélite satellite navigation |

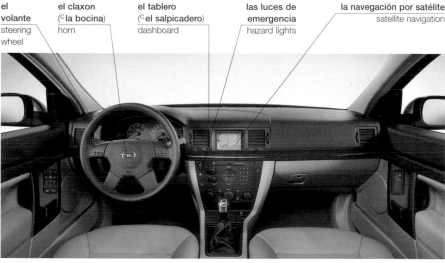

el volante a la izquierda | left-hand drive

el indicador de temperatura
temperature gauge

el tacómetro (^Cel cuentarrevoluciones)
tachometer

el velocímetro (^Cel indicador de velocidad)
speedometer

el indicador de la gasolina
fuel gauge

la radio del coche
car stereo

la palanca (^Cel conmutador) de luces
light switch

la calefacción
heater controls

el odómetro (^Cel cuenta-kilómetros)
odometer

la palanca de velocidades (^Cde cambios)
gearshift

la bolsa de aire (^Cel airbag)
air bag

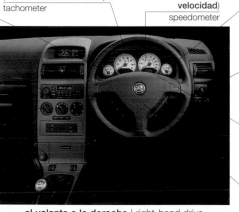

el volante a la derecha | right-hand drive

el carro (^c el coche) 3 • car 3

la mecánica • mechanics

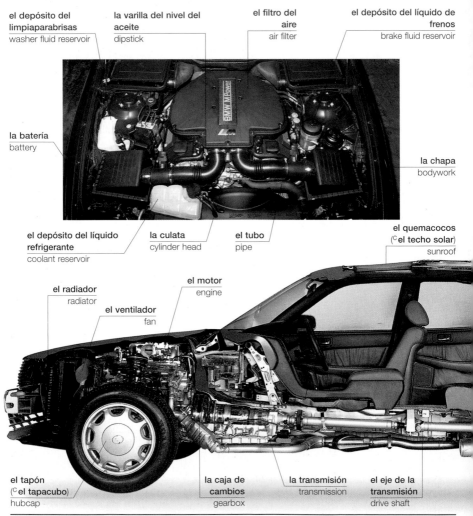

el depósito del limpiaparabrisas
washer fluid reservoir

la varilla del nivel del aceite
dipstick

el filtro del aire
air filter

el depósito del líquido de frenos
brake fluid reservoir

la batería
battery

la chapa
bodywork

el depósito del líquido refrigerante
coolant reservoir

la culata
cylinder head

el tubo
pipe

el quemacocos
(^c el techo solar)
sunroof

el radiador
radiator

el ventilador
fan

el motor
engine

el tapón
(^c el tapacubo)
hubcap

la caja de cambios
gearbox

la transmisión
transmission

el eje de la transmisión
drive shaft

la ponchadura (^cel pinchazo) • flat tire

la llanta de refacción
(^cla rueda de repuesto)
spare tire

la llave
tire iron

los birlos (^clos tornillos)
lug nuts

el gato
jack

cambiar una llanta (^cuna rueda)
change a tire (v)

el techo
roof

la suspensión
suspension

el silenciador
muffler

el tubo de escape
exhaust pipe

vocabulario • vocabulary

el accidente de carro	el tanque de la gasolina
car accident	gas tank
la avería	el turbo
breakdown	turbocharger
el seguro	el distribuidor
insurance	distributor
la grúa	el ralentí
tow truck	timing
el mecánico	el chasis
mechanic	chassis
la presión del neumático	la banda del disco (^cla correa del disco)
tire pressure	cam belt
la caja de fusibles	el freno de mano
fuse box	parking brake
la bujía	la banda del ventilador (^cla correa del ventilador)
spark plug	fan belt
el alternador	
alternator	

Se descompuso el carro.
(^cMi coche se ha averiado.)
My car has broken down.

El carro no arranca.
(^cMi coche no arranca.)
My car won't start.

la motocicleta • motorcycle

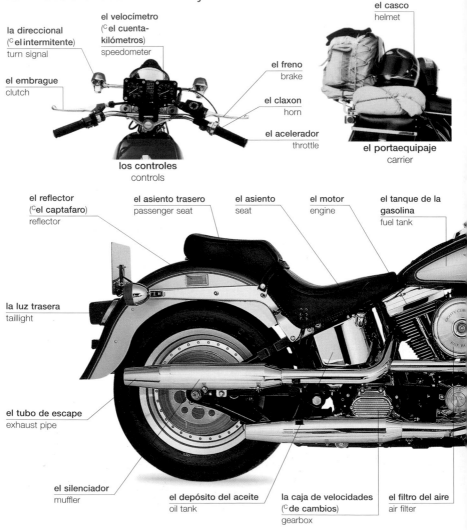

la direccional
(^C el intermitente)
turn signal

el velocímetro
(^C el cuenta-
kilómetros)
speedometer

el casco
helmet

el embrague
clutch

el freno
brake

el claxon
horn

el acelerador
throttle

los controles
controls

el portaequipaje
carrier

el reflector
(^C el captafaro)
reflector

el asiento trasero
passenger seat

el asiento
seat

el motor
engine

el tanque de la
gasolina
fuel tank

la luz trasera
taillight

el tubo de escape
exhaust pipe

el silenciador
muffler

el depósito del aceite
oil tank

la caja de velocidades
(^C de cambios)
gearbox

el filtro del aire
air filter

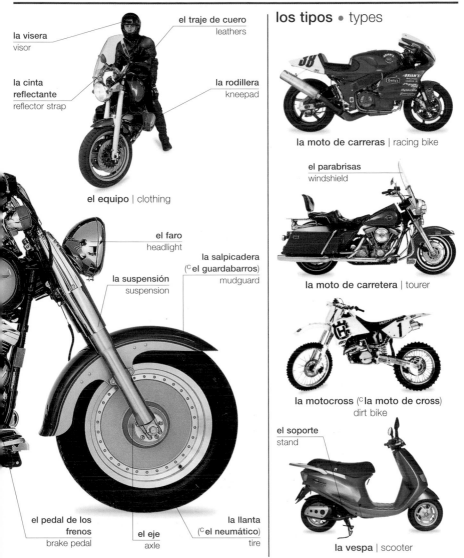

la visera
visor

el traje de cuero
leathers

la cinta reflectante
reflector strap

la rodillera
kneepad

el equipo | clothing

el faro
headlight

la salpicadera
(C **el guardabarros**)
mudguard

la suspensión
suspension

el pedal de los frenos
brake pedal

el eje
axle

la llanta
(C **el neumático**)
tire

los tipos • types

la moto de carreras | racing bike

el parabrisas
windshield

la moto de carretera | tourer

la motocross (C **la moto de cross**)
dirt bike

el soporte
stand

la vespa | scooter

la bicicleta • bicycle

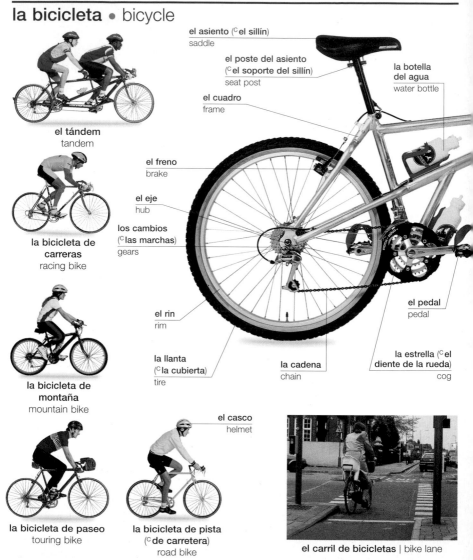

el asiento (^Cel sillín)
saddle

el poste del asiento
(^Cel soporte del sillín)
seat post

la botella
del agua
water bottle

el cuadro
frame

el freno
brake

el eje
hub

los cambios
(^Clas marchas)
gears

el rin
rim

la llanta
(^Cla cubierta)
tire

la cadena
chain

el pedal
pedal

la estrella (^Cel
diente de la rueda)
cog

el tándem
tandem

la bicicleta de
carreras
racing bike

la bicicleta de
montaña
mountain bike

la bicicleta de paseo
touring bike

el casco
helmet

la bicicleta de pista
(^Cde carretera)
road bike

el carril de bicicletas | bike lane

el tubo superior
crossbar

el manubrio
(ᶜel manillar)
handlebar

la palanca de cambio
gear lever

los frenos
brake lever

la palanca
de la llanta
tire lever

el parche
patch

el kit de reparaciones | repair kit

las tijeras
(ᶜla horquilla)
fork

la llave
key

el rayo
(ᶜel radio)
spoke

la bomba
pump

el candado
lock

la llanta
(ᶜla rueda)
wheel

la válvula
valve

la banda de rodadura
tread

la cámara
inner tube

la silla de niños
child seat

---

vocabulario · vocabulary

el faro headlight	el cable cable	el engrane (ᶜel piñón) sprocket	la dinamo dynamo	el calzapié toe clip	frenar brake (v)
el faro trasero rear light	el reflector (ᶜel captafaro) reflector	las ruedas de apoyo training wheels	la canastilla (ᶜla cesta) basket	la banda del calzapié (ᶜla correa del calzapié) toe strap	andar (ᶜir) en bicicleta cycle (v)
la patilla de apoyo kickstand	el rack (ᶜla baca) para bicicletas bike rack	la goma (ᶜel taco) del freno brake block	la ponchadura (ᶜel pinchazo) flat tire	pedalear pedal (v)	cambiar de velocidad (ᶜmarcha) change gear (v)

el tren • train

el vagón
railcar

el andén
platform

el carrito
cart

el número de
andén
platform number

el viajero
de cercanías
commuter

la estación de tren | train station

los tipos de tren • types of train

la cabina del
conductor
engineer's
cab

la locomotora
engine

el riel (ᶜel raíl)
rail

el tren de vapor
steam train

el tren diesel | diesel train

el tren eléctrico
electric train

el tren de alta velocidad
high-speed train

el monorriel (ᶜel monorraíl)
monorail

el metro
subway

el tranvía
tram

el tren de carga
(ᶜel tren de mercancías)
freight train

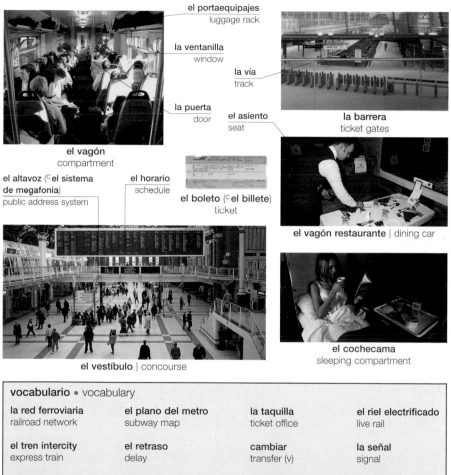

el portaequipajes
luggage rack

la ventanilla
window

la vía
track

la puerta
door

el asiento
seat

la barrera
ticket gates

el vagón
compartment

el altavoz (ᶜel sistema de megafonía)
public address system

el horario
schedule

el boleto (ᶜel billete)
ticket

el vagón restaurante | dining car

el cochecama
sleeping compartment

el vestíbulo | concourse

vocabulario • vocabulary

la red ferroviaria railroad network	**el plano del metro** subway map	**la taquilla** ticket office	**el riel electrificado** live rail
el tren intercity express train	**el retraso** delay	**cambiar** transfer (v)	**la señal** signal
la hora pico (ᶜ**la hora punta**) rush hour	**el precio** fare	**el checador** (ᶜ**el revisor**) ticket inspector	**la palanca de emergencia** emergency lever

el avión • aircraft

el avión de pasajeros • airliner

la nariz
(^C el morro)
nose

la cabina
de pilotaje
cockpit

el motor
engine

el fuselaje
fuselage

el ala
wing

la cola
tail

el timón
rudder

el tren
delantero
nosewheel

la salida
exit

el tren de aterrizaje
landing gear

el alerón
aileron

la aleta
fin

el estabilizador
tailplane

la cabina • cabin

la salida de emergencia
emergency exit

la sobrecargo
(^C la azafata de vuelo)
flight attendant

el compartimento
portaequipajes
overhead bin

la
ventanilla
window

el ventilador
air vent

la luz de lectura
reading light

el asiento
seat

la fila
row

la mesa plegable
(^C la bandeja)
tray-table

el descansabrazos
(^C el apoyabrazos)
armrest

el pasillo
aisle

el respaldo
seat back

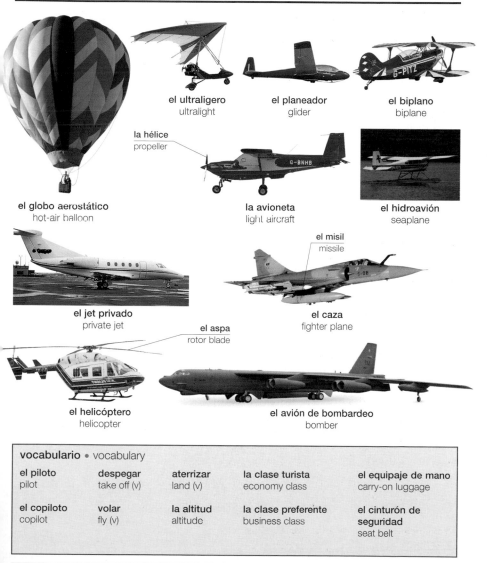

el ultraligero
ultralight

el planeador
glider

el biplano
biplane

la hélice
propeller

el globo aerostático
hot-air balloon

la avioneta
light aircraft

el hidroavión
seaplane

el misil
missile

el jet privado
private jet

el caza
fighter plane

el aspa
rotor blade

el helicóptero
helicopter

el avión de bombardeo
bomber

vocabulario • vocabulary				
el piloto pilot	**despegar** take off (v)	**aterrizar** land (v)	**la clase turista** economy class	**el equipaje de mano** carry-on luggage
el copiloto copilot	**volar** fly (v)	**la altitud** altitude	**la clase preferente** business class	**el cinturón de seguridad** seat belt

el aeropuerto • airport

la pista de estacionamiento
apron

el remolque del equipaje
baggage trailer

la terminal
terminal

el vehículo de servicio
service vehicle

la pasarela
jetway

el avión de línea | airliner

---

vocabulario • vocabulary

la pista runway	**la aduana** customs	**la seguridad** security	**las vacaciones** vacation
el vuelo internacional international flight	**el número de vuelo** flight number	**la banda transportadora** (ᶜla cinta de equipajes) baggage carousel	**reservar un vuelo** book a flight (v)
el vuelo nacional domestic flight	**inmigración** immigration	**la máquina de rayos x** X-ray machine	**la torre de control** control tower (v)
la conexión connection	**el exceso de equipaje** excess baggage	**el folleto de viajes** travel brochure	**hacer check-in** (ᶜfacturar) check in (v)

el equipaje de mano
carry-on luggage

el equipaje
luggage

el carrito
(ᶜel carro)
cart

el mostrador de check-in
(ᶜ**el mostrador de facturación**)
check-in desk

la visa
(ᶜel visado)
visa

el pasaporte | passport

la tarjeta de embarque
boarding pass

el control de pasaportes
passport control

el boleto (ᶜel billete)
ticket

el número de puerta de embarque
gate number

el destino
destination

las llegadas
arrivals

las salidas
departures

la sala de embarque
departure lounge

la pantalla de información
information screen

el duty-free (ᶜ**la tienda libre de impuestos**)
duty-free store

la recogida de equipajes
baggage claim

el sitio de taxis
(ᶜ**la parada de taxis**)
taxi stand

la renta de carros
(ᶜ**el alquiler de coches**)
car rental

el barco • ship

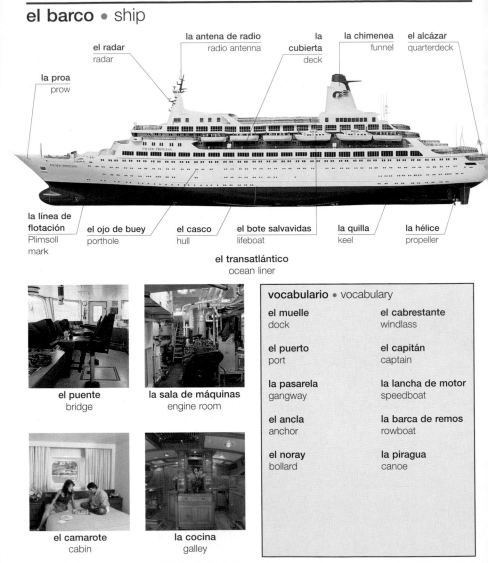

la antena de radio
radio antenna

el radar
radar

la cubierta
deck

la chimenea
funnel

el alcázar
quarterdeck

la proa
prow

la línea de flotación
Plimsoll mark

el ojo de buey
porthole

el casco
hull

el bote salvavidas
lifeboat

la quilla
keel

la hélice
propeller

el transatlántico
ocean liner

el puente
bridge

la sala de máquinas
engine room

vocabulario • vocabulary

el muelle dock	**el cabrestante** windlass
el puerto port	**el capitán** captain
la pasarela gangway	**la lancha de motor** speedboat
el ancla anchor	**la barca de remos** rowboat
el noray bollard	**la piragua** canoe

el camarote
cabin

la cocina
galley

otras embarcaciones • other ships

el ferry
ferry

el motor fueraborda
outboard motor

la zodiac
inflatable dinghy

el hidrodeslizador
hydrofoil

el yate
yacht

el catamarán
catamaran

el remolcador
tugboat

el aerodeslizador
hovercraft

el barco carguero (ᶜel buque portacontenedores)
container ship

las jarcias
rigging

la bodega
hold

el barco de vela
sailboat

el buque de carga
freighter

el buque tanque
(ᶜ**el petrolero**)
oil tanker

el portaaviones
aircraft carrier

el barco de guerra
battleship

la falsa torre
conning tower

el submarino
submarine

el puerto • port

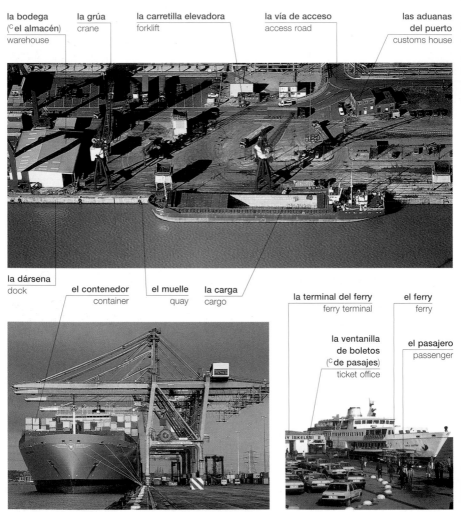

la bodega
(^C el almacén)
warehouse

la grúa
crane

la carretilla elevadora
forklift

la vía de acceso
access road

las aduanas
del puerto
customs house

la dársena
dock

el contenedor
container

el muelle
quay

la carga
cargo

la terminal del ferry
ferry terminal

el ferry
ferry

la ventanilla
de boletos
(^C de pasajes)
ticket office

el pasajero
passenger

el muelle comercial | container port

el muelle de pasajeros | passenger port

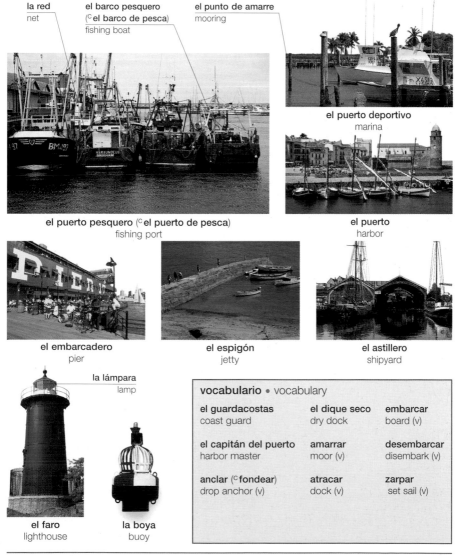

la red
net

el barco pesquero
(ᶜ el barco de pesca)
fishing boat

el punto de amarre
mooring

el puerto deportivo
marina

el puerto pesquero (ᶜ el puerto de pesca)
fishing port

el puerto
harbor

el embarcadero
pier

el espigón
jetty

el astillero
shipyard

la lámpara
lamp

el faro
lighthouse

la boya
buoy

vocabulario • vocabulary

el guardacostas coast guard	el dique seco dry dock	embarcar board (v)
el capitán del puerto harbor master	amarrar moor (v)	desembarcar disembark (v)
anclar (ᶜfondear) drop anchor (v)	atracar dock (v)	zarpar set sail (v)

los deportes
sports

el fútbol americano • football

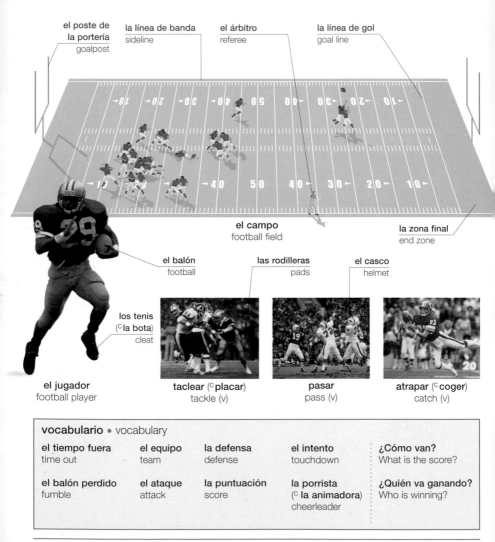

el poste de
la portería
goalpost

la línea de banda
sideline

el árbitro
referee

la línea de gol
goal line

el campo
football field

la zona final
end zone

el balón
football

las rodilleras
pads

el casco
helmet

los tenis
(C la bota)
cleat

el jugador
football player

taclear (C **placar**)
tackle (v)

pasar
pass (v)

atrapar (C **coger**)
catch (v)

vocabulario • vocabulary

el tiempo fuera time out	**el equipo** team	**la defensa** defense	**el intento** touchdown	**¿Cómo van?** What is the score?
el balón perdido fumble	**el ataque** attack	**la puntuación** score	**la porrista** (C **la animadora**) cheerleader	**¿Quién va ganando?** Who is winning?

el rugby • rugby

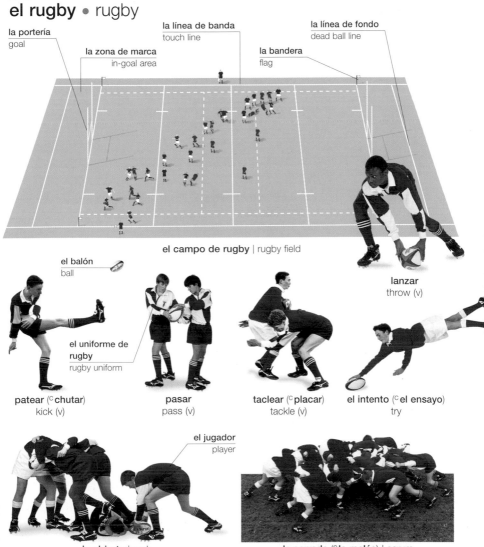

la portería
goal

la línea de banda
touch line

la línea de fondo
dead ball line

la zona de marca
in-goal area

la bandera
flag

el campo de rugby | rugby field

el balón
ball

el uniforme de rugby
rugby uniform

lanzar
throw (v)

patear (c **chutar**)
kick (v)

pasar
pass (v)

taclear (c **placar**)
tackle (v)

el intento (c el ensayo)
try

el jugador
player

la abierta | ruck

la cerrada (c **la melée**) | scrum

el fútbol • soccer

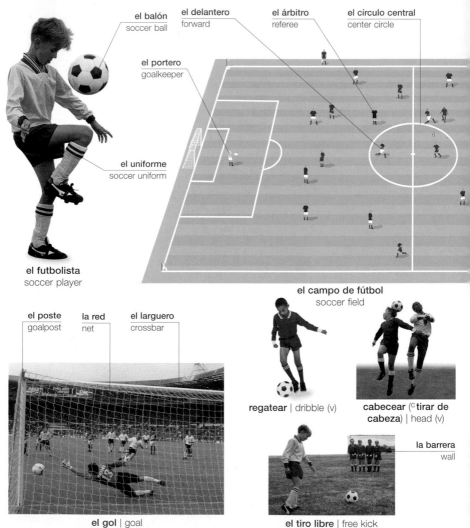

el balón
soccer ball

el delantero
forward

el árbitro
referee

el círculo central
center circle

el portero
goalkeeper

el uniforme
soccer uniform

el futbolista
soccer player

el campo de fútbol
soccer field

el poste
goalpost

la red
net

el larguero
crossbar

regatear | dribble (v)

cabecear (c tirar de cabeza) | head (v)

el gol | goal

la barrera
wall

el tiro libre | free kick

el área de penalti
penalty area

la línea de meta
goal line

el área de meta
goal area

la portería
goal

el defensa
defender

el juez de línea
linesman

la bandera de esquina
corner flag

el saque de banda
throw-in

patear (^{C}chutar)
kick (v)

los tacos
cleat

mandar (^{C}hacer) un pase
pass (v)

tirar
shoot (v)

parar (^{C}hacer una parada)
save (v)

hacer una entrada
tackle (v)

vocabulario • vocabulary

el estadio stadium	la tarjeta amarilla yellow card	la falta foul	la liga league	el reserva substitute
marcar un gol score a goal (v)	la tarjeta roja red card	el fuera de juego offside	el empate tie	el cambio substitution
el penalti penalty	el tiro de esquina (^{C}el córner) corner	la expulsión send off	el descanso halftime	el tiempo extra (^{C}la prórroga) extra time

el hockey • hockey

el hockey sobre hielo • ice hockey

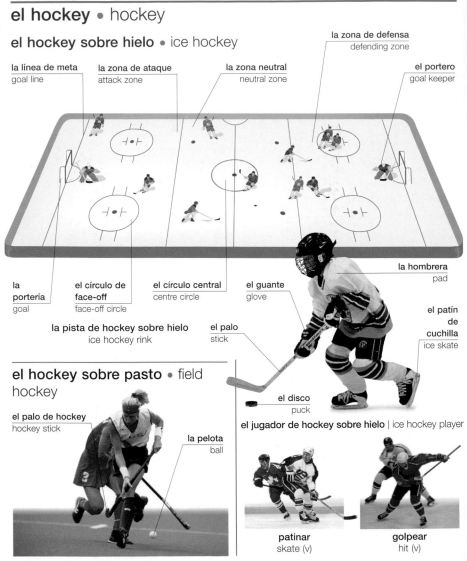

la zona de defensa
defending zone

la línea de meta
goal line

la zona de ataque
attack zone

la zona neutral
neutral zone

el portero
goal keeper

la
portería
goal

el círculo de
face-off
face-off circle

el círculo central
centre circle

el guante
glove

la hombrera
pad

el patín
de
cuchilla
ice skate

la pista de hockey sobre hielo
ice hockey rink

el palo
stick

el hockey sobre pasto • field hockey

el palo de hockey
hockey stick

la pelota
ball

el disco
puck

el jugador de hockey sobre hielo | ice hockey player

patinar
skate (v)

golpear
hit (v)

el críquet • cricket

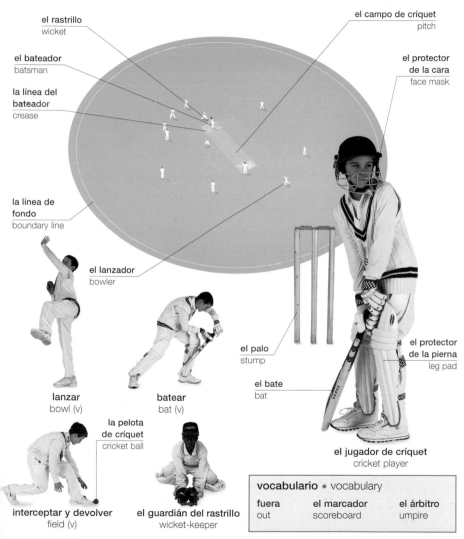

el rastrillo
wicket

el campo de críquet
pitch

el bateador
batsman

el protector
de la cara
face mask

la línea del
bateador
crease

la línea de
fondo
boundary line

el lanzador
bowler

el palo
stump

el protector
de la pierna
leg pad

el bate
bat

lanzar
bowl (v)

batear
bat (v)

la pelota
de críquet
cricket ball

el jugador de críquet
cricket player

interceptar y devolver
field (v)

el guardián del rastrillo
wicket-keeper

vocabulario • vocabulary		
fuera	**el marcador**	**el árbitro**
out	scoreboard	umpire

el baloncesto • basketball

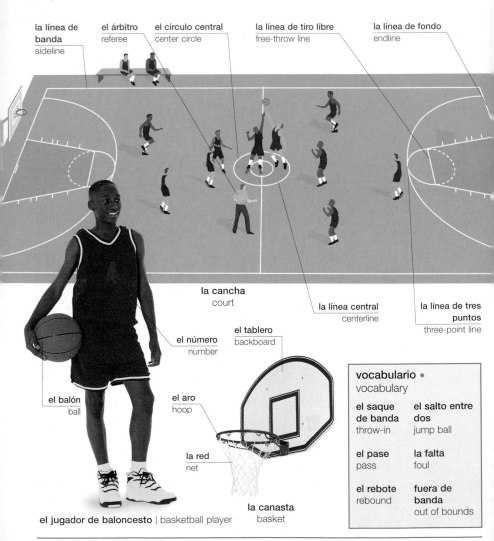

la línea de banda
sideline

el árbitro
referee

el círculo central
center circle

la línea de tiro libre
free-throw line

la línea de fondo
endline

la cancha
court

la línea central
centerline

la línea de tres puntos
three-point line

el número
number

el tablero
backboard

el aro
hoop

la red
net

la canasta
basket

el balón
ball

el jugador de baloncesto | basketball player

vocabulario • vocabulary

el saque de banda throw-in	el salto entre dos jump ball
el pase pass	la falta foul
el rebote rebound	fuera de banda out of bounds

las acciones • actions

lanzar
throw (v)

cachar (ᶜ**coger**)
catch (v)

tirar
shoot (v)

saltar
jump (v)

marcar
mark (v)

bloquear
block (v)

botar
dribble (v)

marcar
dunk (v)

el vóleibol (ᶜ el balonvolea) • volleyball

bloquear
block (v)

la red
net

recibir
dig (v)

el árbitro
referee

la rodillera
knee support

la cancha | court

el béisbol • baseball

el campo • field

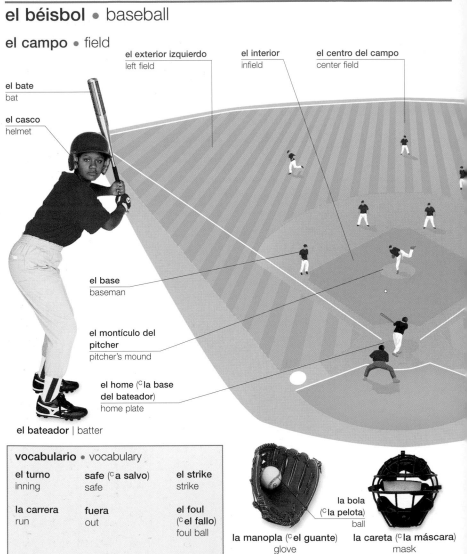

el exterior izquierdo
left field

el interior
infield

el centro del campo
center field

el bate
bat

el casco
helmet

el base
baseman

el montículo del pitcher
pitcher's mound

el home (ᶜla base del bateador)
home plate

el bateador | batter

---

vocabulario • vocabulary

el turno inning	**safe** (ᶜa salvo) safe	**el strike** strike
la carrera run	**fuera** out	**el foul** (ᶜel fallo) foul ball

la bola
(ᶜla pelota)
ball

la manopla (ᶜel guante)
glove

la careta (ᶜla máscara)
mask

las acciones • actions

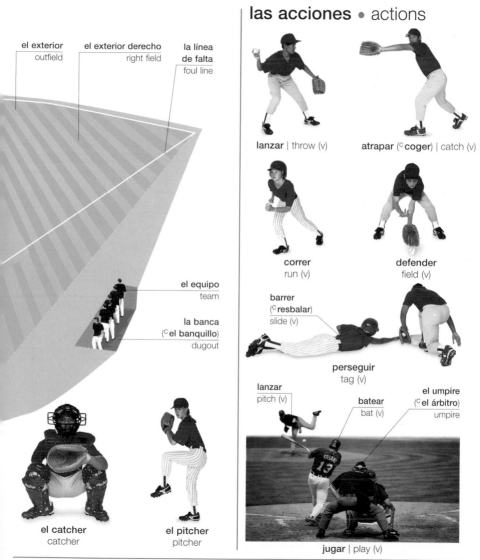

el exterior
outfield

el exterior derecho
right field

la línea
de falta
foul line

el equipo
team

la banca
(C el banquillo)
dugout

el catcher
catcher

el pitcher
pitcher

lanzar | throw (v)

atrapar (C coger) | catch (v)

correr
run (v)

defender
field (v)

barrer
(C resbalar)
slide (v)

perseguir
tag (v)

lanzar
pitch (v)

batear
bat (v)

el umpire
(C el árbitro)
umpire

jugar | play (v)

el tenis • tennis

el mango
handle

la cabeza
head

la cuerda
string

el juez de silla
umpire

la línea de fondo
baseline

la raqueta
racquet

la línea de servicio
service line

la línea de banda
sideline

la bola
(ᶜla pelota)
ball

la muñequera
wristband

la pista de tenis | tennis court

vocabulario • vocabulary

el juego game	**el set** set	**nada** love	**la falta** fault	**el peloteo** rally	**el efecto** spin
los dobles doubles	**el partido** match	**la ventaja** advantage	**el as** ace	**¡red!** let!	**el juez de línea** linesman
el singles (ᶜ**el individual**) singles	**el tiebreak** tiebreaker	**cuarenta iguales** deuce	**la dejada** dropshot	**el tiro con efecto** slice	**el campeonato** championship

los golpes • strokes

la red
net

el remate (^Cel mate)
smash

el recogebolas
(^Cel recogepelotas)
ball boy

sacar
serve (v)

los tenis
tennis shoes

el jugador
player

el servicio
serve

la volea
volley

el resto
return

el globo
lob

el derecho
forehand

el revés
backhand

los juegos de raqueta • racket games

el gallo
(^Cel volante)
shuttlecock

la raqueta
(^Cla pala)
paddle

el bádminton
badminton

el ping-pong
table tennis

el squash
squash

el racketball
racquetball

el golf • golf

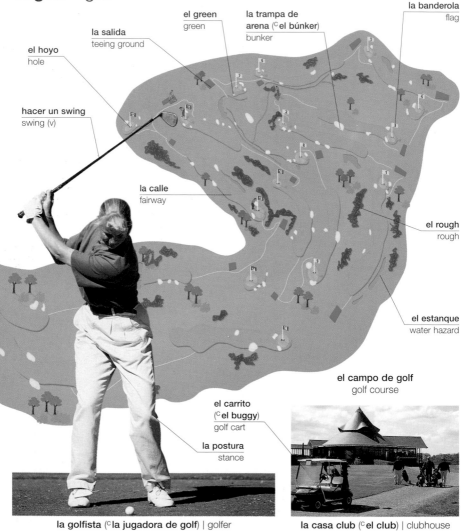

el green
green

la trampa de
arena (^Cel búnker)
bunker

la banderola
flag

la salida
teeing ground

el hoyo
hole

hacer un swing
swing (v)

la calle
fairway

el rough
rough

el estanque
water hazard

el campo de golf
golf course

el carrito
(^Cel buggy)
golf cart

la postura
stance

la golfista (^C**la jugadora de golf**) | golfer

la casa club (^C**el club**) | clubhouse

el equipo • equipment

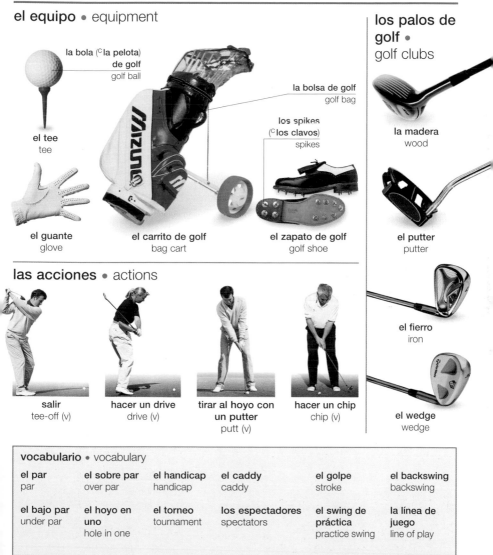

la bola (ᶜla pelota)
de golf
golf ball

el tee
tee

la bolsa de golf
golf bag

los spikes
(ᶜlos clavos)
spikes

el guante
glove

el carrito de golf
bag cart

el zapato de golf
golf shoe

los palos de golf • golf clubs

la madera
wood

el putter
putter

el fierro
iron

el wedge
wedge

las acciones • actions

salir
tee-off (v)

hacer un drive
drive (v)

**tirar al hoyo con
un putter**
putt (v)

hacer un chip
chip (v)

vocabulario • vocabulary

el par par	**el sobre par** over par	**el handicap** handicap	**el caddy** caddy	**el golpe** stroke	**el backswing** backswing
el bajo par under par	**el hoyo en uno** hole in one	**el torneo** tournament	**los espectadores** spectators	**el swing de práctica** practice swing	**la línea de juego** line of play

el atletismo • track and field

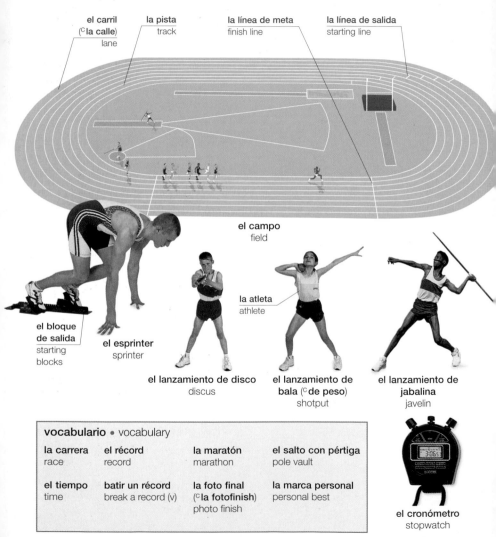

el carril
(ᶜ la calle)
lane

la pista
track

la línea de meta
finish line

la línea de salida
starting line

el campo
field

la atleta
athlete

el bloque
de salida
starting
blocks

el esprinter
sprinter

el lanzamiento de disco
discus

el lanzamiento de
bala (ᶜ de peso)
shotput

el lanzamiento de
jabalina
javelin

vocabulario • vocabulary			
la carrera race	el récord record	la maratón marathon	el salto con pértiga pole vault
el tiempo time	batir un récord break a record (v)	la foto final (ᶜ la fotofinish) photo finish	la marca personal personal best

el cronómetro
stopwatch

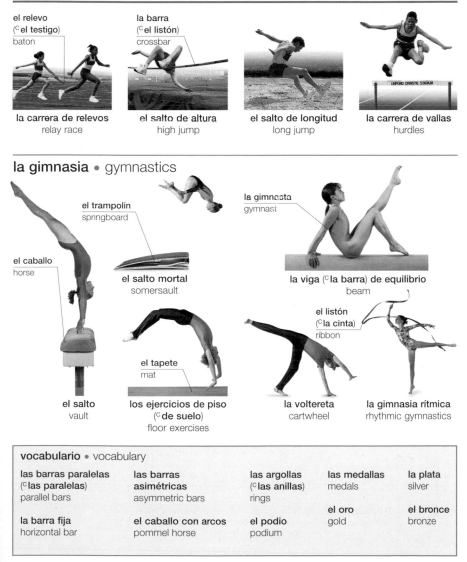

el relevo
(^Cel testigo)
baton

la barra
(^Cel listón)
crossbar

la carrera de relevos
relay race

el salto de altura
high jump

el salto de longitud
long jump

la carrera de vallas
hurdles

la gimnasia • gymnastics

el trampolín
springboard

la gimnasta
gymnast

el caballo
horse

el salto mortal
somersault

la viga (^Cla barra) de equilibrio
beam

el listón
(^Cla cinta)
ribbon

el tapete
mat

el salto
vault

los ejercicios de piso
(^Cde suelo)
floor exercises

la voltereta
cartwheel

la gimnasia rítmica
rhythmic gymnastics

vocabulario • vocabulary

las barras paralelas (^C**las paralelas**) parallel bars	**las barras asimétricas** asymmetric bars	**las argollas** (^C**las anillas**) rings	**las medallas** medals	**la plata** silver
la barra fija horizontal bar	**el caballo con arcos** pommel horse	**el podio** podium	**el oro** gold	**el bronce** bronze

los deportes de combate • combat sports

el adversario
opponent

el protector
guard

el guante
glove

el cinturón
belt

el taekwondo
tae kwon do

el karate
karate

el judo
judo

la careta
mask

la espada
sword

el aikido
aikido

el kendo
kendo

el kung fu
kung fu

el full contact
kickboxing

la lucha libre
wrestling

el boxeo
boxing

los movimientos • actions

la caída
fall

el agarre
hold

el derribo
throw

la inmovilización
pin

la patada
kick

el puñetazo
punch

el golpe
strike

el salto
jump

el bloqueo (ᶜ**la parada**)
block

el golpe
chop

vocabulario • vocabulary

el ring boxing ring	**el combate** bout	**el puño** fist	**el cinturón negro** black belt	**la capoeira** capoeira
los guantes de boxeo boxing gloves	**el round** (ᶜ**el asalto**) round	**el K.O.** knockout	**la defensa personal** self-defense	**el sumo** sumo wrestling
el protegedientes mouth guard	**el entrenamiento** sparring	**el saco de arena** punching bag	**las artes marciales** martial arts	**el tai-chi** tai chi

la natación • swimming
el equipo • equipment

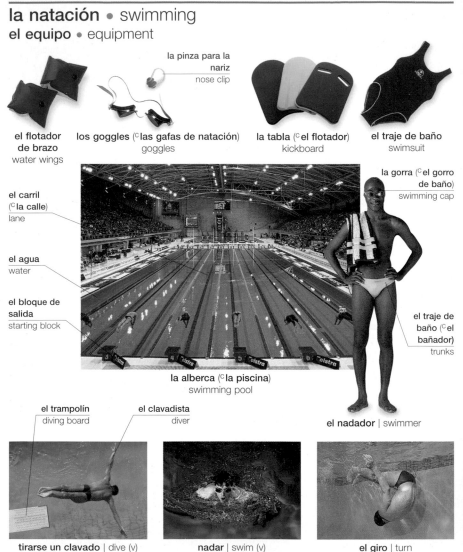

la pinza para la nariz
nose clip

el flotador de brazo
water wings

los goggles (^clas gafas de natación)
goggles

la tabla (^cel flotador)
kickboard

el traje de baño
swimsuit

la gorra (^cel gorro de baño)
swimming cap

el carril (^cla calle)
lane

el agua
water

el bloque de salida
starting block

el traje de baño (^cel bañador)
trunks

la alberca (^cla piscina)
swimming pool

el nadador | swimmer

el trampolín
diving board

el clavadista
diver

tirarse un clavado | dive (v)

nadar | swim (v)

el giro | turn

los estilos • styles

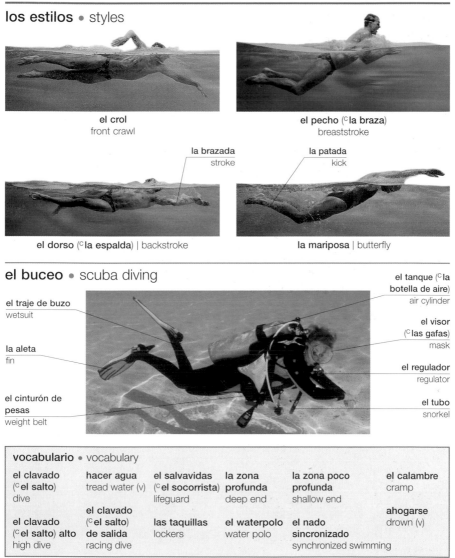

el crol
front crawl

el pecho (C **la braza**)
breaststroke

la brazada
stroke

la patada
kick

el dorso (C **la espalda**) | backstroke

la mariposa | butterfly

el buceo • scuba diving

el tanque (C la
botella de aire)
air cylinder

el traje de buzo
wetsuit

el visor
(C las gafas)
mask

la aleta
fin

el regulador
regulator

el cinturón de
pesas
weight belt

el tubo
snorkel

---

vocabulario • vocabulary

el clavado (C **el salto**) dive	**hacer agua** tread water (v)	**el salvavidas** (C **el socorrista**) lifeguard	**la zona profunda** deep end	**la zona poco profunda** shallow end	**el calambre** cramp
el clavado (C **el salto**) **alto** high dive	**el clavado** (C **el salto**) **de salida** racing dive	**las taquillas** lockers	**el waterpolo** water polo	**el nado sincronizado** synchronized swimming	**ahogarse** drown (v)

la vela • sailing

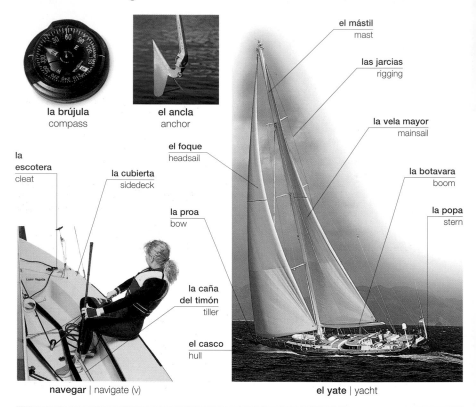

la brújula
compass

el ancla
anchor

el mástil
mast

las jarcias
rigging

la vela mayor
mainsail

la botavara
boom

la popa
stern

el foque
headsail

la escotera
cleat

la cubierta
sidedeck

la proa
bow

la caña del timón
tiller

el casco
hull

navegar | navigate (v)

el yate | yacht

la seguridad • safety

la bengala
flare

el salvavidas
life buoy

el chaleco salvavidas
life jacket

la balsa salvavidas
life raft

los deportes acuáticos • watersports

el remero
rower

el remo
oar

el kayak
kayak

el remo
paddle

remar | row (v)

hacer kayak
kayaking

la vela
sail

la tabla
de surf
surfboard

el esquí
waterski

el
windsurfista
windsurfer

el surfing
surfing

el esquí acuático
waterskiing

la carrera de lanchas
(ᶜ **de motoras**)
speedboating

la tabla
board

la cinta para el pie
footstrap

el windsurf | windsurfing

el rafting
rafting

la moto acuática
jet skiing

---

vocabulario • vocabulary

el surfista surfer	**la tripulación** crew	**el viento** wind	**la rompiente** surf	**la escota** sheet	**la orza** centerboard
el esquiador acuático waterskier	**virar** tack (v)	**la ola** wave	**los rápidos** rapids	**el timón** rudder	**volcar** capsize (v)

---

la equitación • horseback riding

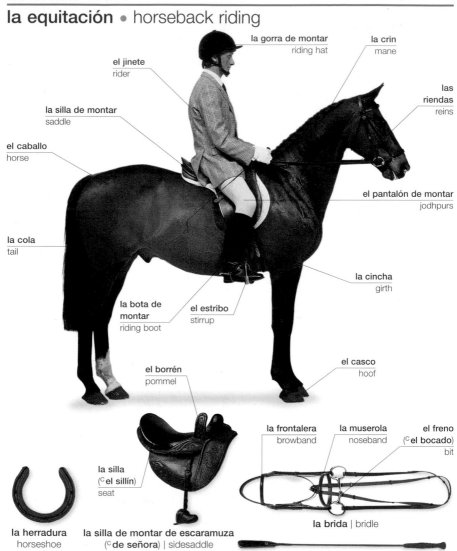

la gorra de montar
riding hat

la crin
mane

el jinete
rider

las riendas
reins

la silla de montar
saddle

el caballo
horse

el pantalón de montar
jodhpurs

la cola
tail

la cincha
girth

la bota de montar
riding boot

el estribo
stirrup

el casco
hoof

el borrén
pommel

la frontalera
browband

la muserola
noseband

el freno
(C el bocado)
bit

la silla
(C el sillín)
seat

la brida | bridle

la herradura
horseshoe

la silla de montar de escaramuza
(C de señora) | sidesaddle

la fusta | riding crop

las modalidades • events

el caballo de carreras
racehorse

la valla
fence

la carrera de caballos
horse race

la carrera de obstáculos
steeplechase

la carrera al trote
harness race

el rodeo
rodeo

el concurso de saltos
show jumping

la carrera de carrozas
carriage race

el paseo
trail riding

la doma y monta
dressage

el polo
polo

---

vocabulario • vocabulary

el paso walk	**el medio galope** canter	**el salto** jump	**el cabestro** halter	**el cercado** paddock	**el hipódromo** racecourse
el trote trot	**el galope** gallop	**el mozo de cuadra** groom	**la cuadra** stable	**el ruedo** arena	**la carrera sin obstáculos** flat race

---

la pesca • fishing

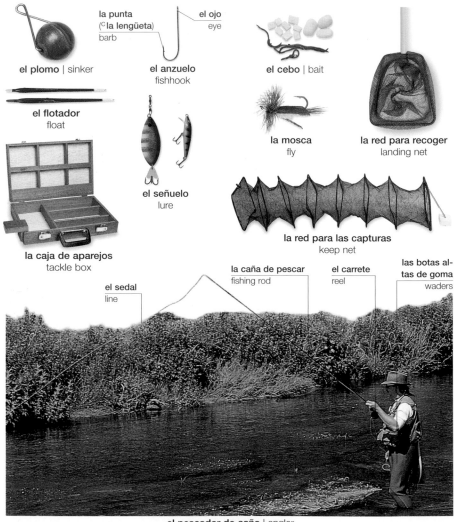

el plomo | sinker

la punta
(^Cla lengüeta)
barb

el ojo
eye

el anzuelo
fishhook

el cebo | bait

la mosca
fly

la red para recoger
landing net

el flotador
float

el señuelo
lure

la caja de aparejos
tackle box

la red para las capturas
keep net

la caña de pescar
fishing rod

el carrete
reel

**las botas al-
tas de goma**
waders

el sedal
line

el pescador de caña | angler

los tipos de pesca • types of fishing

la pesca en agua dulce
freshwater fishing

la pesca con mosca
fly fishing

la pesca deportiva
sport fishing

la pesca de altura
deep sea fishing

la pesca en la orilla
surfcasting

las acciones • activities

lanzar
cast (v)

atrapar (ᶜcoger)
catch (v)

recoger
reel in (v)

atrapar (ᶜcoger)
con la red
net (v)

soltar
release (v)

---

vocabulario • vocabulary

cebar bait (v)	**los aparejos** tackle	**la ropa impermeable** rain gear	**la licencia de pesca** fishing license	**la nasa** creel
picar bite (v)	**el carrete** spool	**la pértiga** pole	**la pesca en alta mar** marine fishing	**la pesca con arpón** spearfishing

---

el esquí · skiing

la pista
ski slope

la telesilla
chairlift

la góndola
(^Cel teleférico)
cable car

el guante
glove

el bastón
ski pole

la punta
tip

el canto
edge

el esquí
ski

la pista de esquí
ski run

la barrera de
seguridad
safety barrier

la chaqueta de
esquí
ski jacket

la esquiadora
skier

la bota de esquí
ski boot

las modalidades • events

el poste
gate

el descenso
downhill skiing

el slalom
slalom

el salto
ski jump

el esquí de fondo
cross-country skiing

los deportes de invierno • winter sports

los goggles
(ᶜ **las gafas**)
goggles

el patín
skate

la escalada en hielo
ice climbing

el patinaje sobre hielo
ice-skating

el patinaje artístico
figure skating

el snowboarding
snowboarding

el bobsleigh
bobsled

el luge
luge

la moto de nieve
snowmobile

tirarse en trineo
sledding

---

vocabulario • vocabulary

el esquí alpino
alpine skiing

el trineo con perros
dogsledding

el slalom gigante
giant slalom

el biatlón
biathlon

fuera de pista
off-piste

la avalancha
avalanche

el curling
curling

el patinaje de velocidad
speed skating

los otros deportes • other sports

el planeador
glider

el ala delta
hang-glider

el vuelo sin motor
gliding

el paracaídas
parachute

el vuelo con ala delta
hang-gliding

la cuerda
rope

la escalada
rock climbing

el paracaidismo
parachuting

el parapente
paragliding

el paracaidismo en caída libre
skydiving

el rappel
rappelling

el salto bungee (ᶜel puenting)
bungee jumping

el rally
rally driving

**el piloto
de carreras**
race-car
driver

el automovilismo
auto racing

el motocross
motocross

el motociclismo
motorcycle racing

la patineta
(ᶜ**el monopatín**)
skateboard

andar en patineta
(ᶜ**montar en monopatín**)
skateboarding

el patinaje en línea
inline skating

el palo
stick

el lacrosse
lacrosse

**la
máscara**
mask

el florete
foil

el esgrima
fencing

el pino (ᶜ**el bolo**)
pin

el arco
bow

la flecha
arrow

el carcaj
quiver

la diana
target

el tiro con arco
archery

el tiro
target shooting

**la bola
de boliche**
(ᶜ**de bowling**)
bowling ball

el boliche (ᶜ**los bolos**)
bowling

el pool (ᶜ**el billar
americano**) | pool

el billar
snooker

la forma física • fitness

la bicicleta
exercise bike

la máquina de ejercicios
gym machine

el banco
bench

las pesas
free weights

la barra
bar

el gimasio
gym

la máquina de remos
rowing machine

la banda caminadora
treadmill

la máquina de cross
elliptical trainer

la entrenadora personal
personal trainer

la máquina de step
stair machine

la alberca
(ᶜla piscina)
swimming pool

el sauna
sauna

los ejercicios • exercises

el estiramiento
stretch

la flexión con estiramiento
lunge

los leotardos
tights

la flexión
push-up

la pesa
dumbbell

el abdominal
sit-up

el ejercicio de bíceps
bicep curl

los ejercicios de piernas
leg press

ponerse en cuclillas
squat

las zapatillas
sneakers

la barra de pesas
weight bar

los ejercicios pectorales
chest press

el levantamiento de pesas
weight training

el jogging
(ᶜel footing)
jogging

el pilates
Pilates

vocabulario • vocabulary

entrenar train (v)	**correr en parada** jog in place (v)	**estirar** extend (v)	**la gimnasia prepugilística** boxercise	**saltar a la comba** jumping rope
calentar warm up (v)	**flexionar** flex (v)	**levantar** pull up (v)	**el entrenamiento en circuito** circuit training	

el ocio
leisure

el teatro • theater

el telón
curtain

los bastidores
wings

la escenografía
(^C el decorado)
set

el público
audience

la orquesta
orchestra

el escenario | stage

la butaca
seat

la platea alta
balcony

la fila
row

el palco
box

la platea
mezzanine

la galería
balcony

el pasillo
aisle

las butacas
generales
(^C el patio
de butacas)
seats

las butacas | seating

vocabulario • vocabulary

la obra play	el director director	el estreno opening night
el reparto cast	el productor producer	el programa program
el actor actor	el guión script	el foso de la orquesta orchestra pit
la actriz actress	el telón de fondo backdrop	el entreacto (^C el descanso) intermission

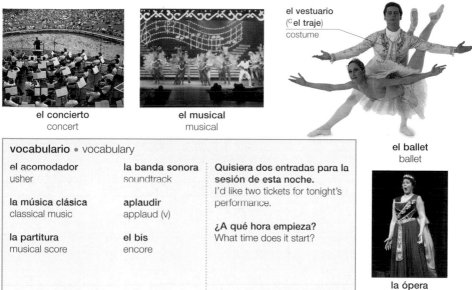

el concierto
concert

el musical
musical

el vestuario
(^C **el traje**)
costume

el ballet
ballet

la ópera
opera

vocabulario • vocabulary

el acomodador
usher

la música clásica
classical music

la partitura
musical score

la banda sonora
soundtrack

aplaudir
applaud (v)

el bis
encore

Quisiera dos entradas para la sesión de esta noche.
I'd like two tickets for tonight's performance.

¿A qué hora empieza?
What time does it start?

el cine • movies

las palomitas
popcorn

la taquilla
box office

el vestíbulo
lobby

el póster
poster

el cine
movie theater

la pantalla
screen

vocabulario • vocabulary

la comedia
comedy

la película de suspense
thriller

la película de miedo
horror movie

la película de vaqueros (^C **del oeste**)
Western

la película romántica
romance

la película de ciencia ficción
science fiction movie

la película de aventuras
adventure movie

la película de dibujos animados
animated movie

la orquesta • orchestra

la cuerda • strings

el arpa
harp

el director de orquesta
conductor

el contrabajo
double bass

el violín
violin

el podio
podium

la viola
viola

el violoncelo
cello

la partitura
score

la clave de sol
treble clef

la nota
note

el pentagrama
staff

la clave de fa
bass clef

el piano | piano

la notación | notation

vocabulario • vocabulary

la obertura overture	**la sonata** sonata	**la pausa** rest	**sostenido** sharp	**el becuadro** natural	**la escala** scale
la sinfonía symphony	**los instrumentos** instruments	**el tono** pitch	**bemol** flat	**el compás** bar	**la batuta** baton

el viento-madera • woodwind

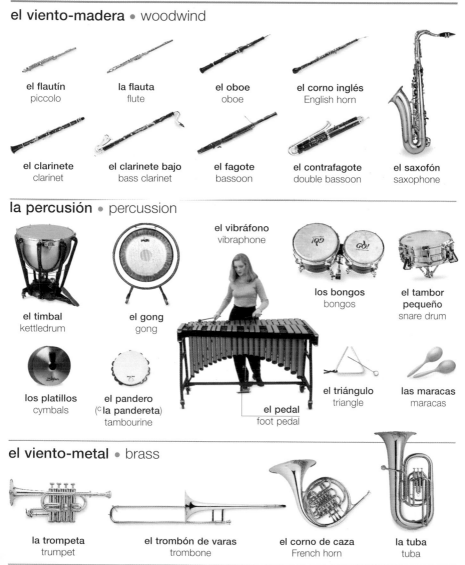

el flautín
piccolo

la flauta
flute

el oboe
oboe

el corno inglés
English horn

el clarinete
clarinet

el clarinete bajo
bass clarinet

el fagote
bassoon

el contrafagote
double bassoon

el saxofón
saxophone

la percusión • percussion

el vibráfono
vibraphone

los bongos
bongos

el tambor
pequeño
snare drum

el timbal
kettledrum

el gong
gong

los platillos
cymbals

el pandero
(ᶜ la pandereta)
tambourine

el pedal
foot pedal

el triángulo
triangle

las maracas
maracas

el viento-metal • brass

la trompeta
trumpet

el trombón de varas
trombone

el corno de caza
French horn

la tuba
tuba

el concierto • concert

la bocina
(^Cel altavoz)
speaker

los fans
fans

el vocalista
(^Cel cantante)
lead singer

el guitarrista
guitarist

el micrófono
microphone

el baterista
(^Cel batería)
drummer

el concierto de rock | rock concert

los instrumentos • instruments

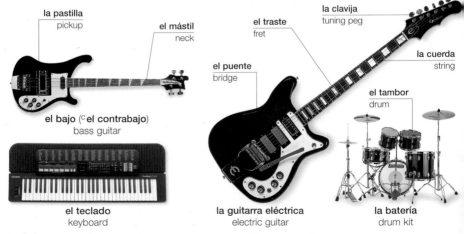

la pastilla
pickup

el mástil
neck

el traste
fret

la clavija
tuning peg

la cuerda
string

el puente
bridge

el tambor
drum

el bajo (^C**el contrabajo**)
bass guitar

el teclado
keyboard

la guitarra eléctrica
electric guitar

la batería
drum kit

los estilos musicales • musical styles

el jazz
jazz

el blues
blues

el punk
punk

la música folklórica (ᶜfolk)
folk music

el pop
pop

la música de baile
dance

el rap
rap

el heavy metal
heavy metal

la música clásica
classical music

---

vocabulario • vocabulary

la canción	**la letra**	**la melodía**	**el ritmo**	**el reggae**	**la música country**	**el reflector** (ᶜel foco)
song	lyrics	melody	beat	reggae	country	spotlight

---

el turismo • sightseeing

el
itinerario
itinerary

descubierto
open-top

el autobús turístico | tour bus

el turista
tourist

la atracción turística | tourist attraction

el guío
turístico
tour guide

la estatuilla
figurine

la visita guiada
(ᶜ **la visita con guía**)
guided tour

los recuerdos
souvenirs

---

vocabulario • vocabulary

el precio de entrada entrance fee	**la guía del viajero** guidebook	**la película** film	**la izquierda** left	**¿Dónde está…?** Where is…?
abierto open	**la cámara de vídeo** camcorder	**la cámara** (ᶜ **la máquina**) **fotográfica** camera	**la derecha** right	**Estoy perdido.** (ᶜ **Me he perdido.**) I'm lost.
cerrado closed	**las pilas** batteries	**las indicaciones** directions	**recto** straight ahead	**¿Podría decirme cómo se va a…?** Can you tell me the way to…?

los lugares de interés • attractions

el cuadro
painting

la muestra
exhibit

la exposición
exhibition

la ruina famosa
famous ruin

la galería de arte
art gallery

el monumento
monument

el museo
museum

el edificio histórico
historic building

el casino
casino

los jardines
gardens

el parque nacional
national park

la información • information

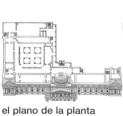

las horas
times

el plano de la planta
floor plan

el mapa (ᶜ el plano)
map

el horario
schedule

la oficina de información
tourist information

las actividades al aire libre • outdoor activities

el
sendero
footpath

el reloj de sol
sundial

la cafetería
café

el parque | park

el **pasto**
(ᶜ **la hierba**)
grass

la banca
(ᶜ **el banco**)
bench

los **jardines**
clásicos
formal gardens

la montaña rusa
roller coaster

la feria
fairground

el parque de diversiones
(ᶜ **el parque de atracciones**)
theme park

el safari park
safari park

el zoológico (ᶜ **el zoo**)
zoo

las actividades • activities

el ciclismo
cycling

el jogging
jogging

la patineta
(^{C}**montar en patinete**)
skateboarding

el patinaje
rollerblading

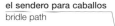

el sendero para caballos
bridle path

la ornitología
bird-watching

la equitación
horseback riding

la caminata
(^{C}**el senderismo**)
hiking

la canasta
(^{C}**la cesta**)
hamper

el picnic
picnic

el área de juegos • playground

el cajón de arena
sandbox

la alberca (^{C}la piscina)
de plástico
wading pool

los columpios
swing

el subibaja | seesaw

la resbaladilla (^{C}el tobogán)
slide

el changuero
(^{C}**la estructura para escalar**)
climbing frame

la playa • beach

el hotel
hotel

la sombrilla
beach umbrella

la caseta
beach hut

la arena
sand

la ola
wave

el mar
sea

la bolsa de playa
beach bag

el bikini
bikini

asolear (^C**tomar el sol**) | sunbathe (v)

el salvavidas
(ᶜ **el socorrista**)
lifeguard

la torre de vigilancia
lifeguard tower

la barrera contra el viento
windbreak

el paseo marítimo
boardwalk

el asoleadero (ᶜ**la hamaca**)
deck chair

los lentes obscuros
(ᶜ**las gafas de sol**)
sunglasses

el sombrero para el sol
sun hat

el bronceador
(ᶜ**la crema bronceadora**)
suntan lotion

la crema protectora
sunblock

la pelota de playa
beach ball

la llanta (ᶜ**el flotador**)
inflatable ring

el traje de baño
(ᶜ**el bañador**)
swimsuit

la pala
shovel

la cubeta
(ᶜ**el cubo**)
pail

el castillo de arena
sandcastle

la concha
shell

la toalla de playa
beach towel

el camping • camping

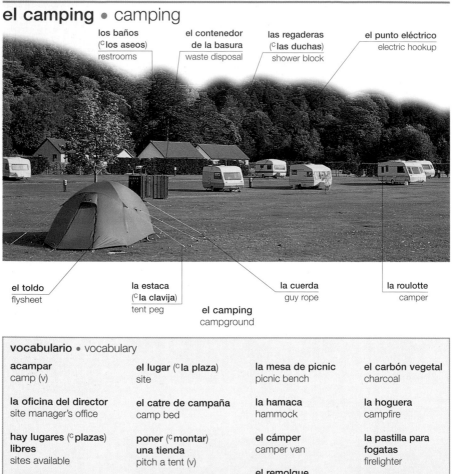

los baños
(ᶜlos aseos)
restrooms

el contenedor
de la basura
waste disposal

las regaderas
(ᶜlas duchas)
shower block

el punto eléctrico
electric hookup

el toldo
flysheet

la estaca
(ᶜla clavija)
tent peg

la cuerda
guy rope

la roulotte
camper

el camping
campground

vocabulario • vocabulary

acampar
camp (v)

la oficina del director
site manager's office

hay lugares (ᶜplazas)
libres
sites available

lleno (ᶜcompleto)
full

el lugar (ᶜla plaza)
site

el catre de campaña
camp bed

poner (ᶜmontar)
una tienda
pitch a tent (v)

el tubo (ᶜel palo) de
la tienda
tent pole

la mesa de picnic
picnic bench

la hamaca
hammock

el cámper
camper van

el remolque
trailer

el carbón vegetal
charcoal

la hoguera
campfire

la pastilla para
fogatas
firelighter

encender una
fogata
light a fire (v)

la estructura
frame

el suelo aislante
ground sheet

la mochila
backpack

el termo
vacuum flask

la cantimplora
water bottle

la tienda de campaña
tent

el repelente (contra insectos)
insect repellent

la linterna
flashlight

el mosquitero
mosquito net

la ropa térmica
(ᶜ**termoaislante**)
thermal underwear

las botas de trekking
hiking boots

la manga
(ᶜ**la ropa impermeable**)
rain gear

el saco de dormir
sleeping bag

la estufilla (ᶜ**el hornillo**)
camping stove

la parrilla (ᶜ**la barbacoa**)
barbecue grill

la esterilla
sleeping mat

la colchoneta | air mattress

el entretenimiento (ᶜel ocio) en el hogar • home entertainment

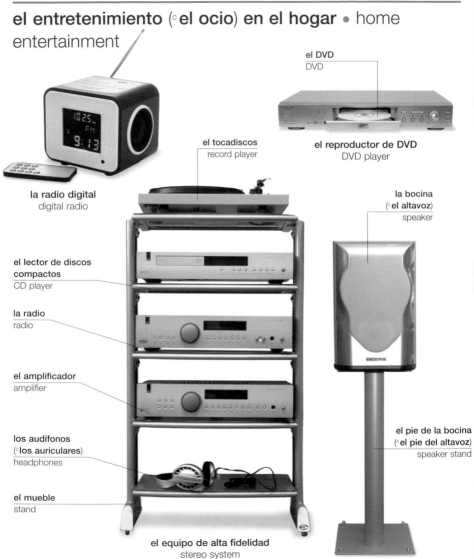

el DVD
DVD

el reproductor de DVD
DVD player

el tocadiscos
record player

la radio digital
digital radio

la bocina
(ᶜel altavoz)
speaker

el lector de discos compactos
CD player

la radio
radio

el amplificador
amplifier

los audífonos
(ᶜlos auriculares)
headphones

el pie de la bocina
(ᶜel pie del altavoz)
speaker stand

el mueble
stand

el equipo de alta fidelidad
stereo system

la pantalla
screen

el borde del ocular
eyecup

el sintonizador digital
DTV converter box

la cámara de vídeo
camcorder

la antena parabólica
satellite dish

el televisor de
pantalla plana
flatscreen TV

la consola
console

el avance rápid
fast-forward

la pausa
pause

el botón para
grabar
record

el volumen
volume

los controles
controller

el botón para rebobinar
rewind

el play
play

el stop
stop

el videojuego | video game

el control remoto (ᵉel mando a distancia)
remote control

vocabulario • vocabulary

el disco compacto CD	estéreo stereo	la casetera (ᵉel magnetofóno) cassette player	el WIFI Wi-Fi	ver la televisión watch television (v)
el casete cassette tape	el anuncio advertisement	la televisión por cable cable television	la película (ᵉel largometraje) feature film	apagar la televisión turn off the television (v)
el programa program	la transmisión por secuencias streaming	el canal de pago por evento pay-per-view channel	cambiar de canal change channel (v)	sintonizar la radio tune the radio (v)
digital digital	alta definición high-definition		encender la televisión turn on the television (v)	

la fotografía • photography

el disparador
shutter release

el obturador
(ᶜla rueda del diafragma)
aperture dial

el lente
(ᶜel objetivo)
lens

la cámara réflex | SLR camera

el filtro
filter

la tapa del lente
(ᶜobjetivo)
lens cap

el flash electrónico
flash gun

el fotómetro
light meter

el zoom (ᶜel teleobjetivo)
zoom lens

el tripié (ᶜel trípode)
tripod

los tipos de cámara • types of camera

el flash
flash

la cámara Polaroid
Polaroid camera

la cámara digital
digital camera

el teléfono con cámara
camera phone

la cámara desechable
disposable camera

fotografiar • photograph (v)

el carrete
film roll

la película
film

enfocar
focus (v)

revelar
develop (v)

el negativo
negative

apaisado
landscape

en formato vertical
portrait

la fotografía | photograph

el álbum de fotos
photo album

el portarretratos
picture frame

los problemas • problems

subexpuesto
underexposed

sobreexpuesto
overexposed

desenfocado
out of focus

los ojos rojos
red eye

vocabulario • vocabulary

el visor viewfinder	**la copia** print
la funda de la cámara camera case	**mate** matte
la exposición exposure	**con brillo** gloss
el cuarto oscuro darkroom	**la ampliación** enlargement

Me gustaría revelar este rollo.
I'd like this film processed.

los juegos • games

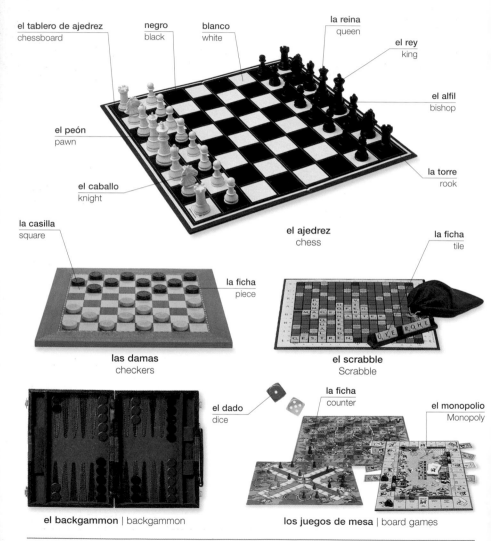

el tablero de ajedrez
chessboard

negro
black

blanco
white

la reina
queen

el rey
king

el alfil
bishop

el peón
pawn

el caballo
knight

la torre
rook

la casilla
square

el ajedrez
chess

la ficha
tile

la ficha
piece

las damas
checkers

el scrabble
Scrabble

el dado
dice

la ficha
counter

el monopolio
Monopoly

el backgammon | backgammon

los juegos de mesa | board games

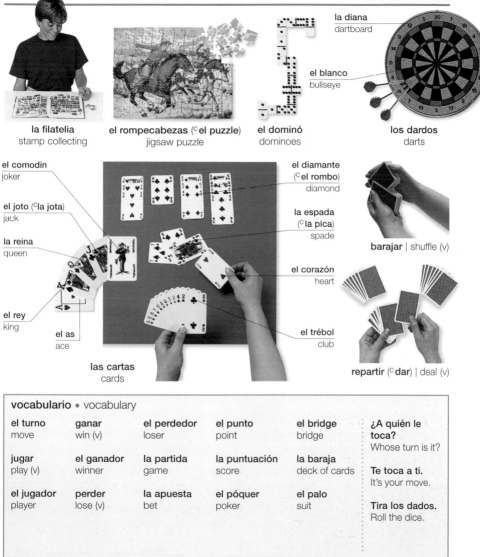

la diana
dartboard

el blanco
bullseye

la filatelia
stamp collecting

el rompecabezas (^C**el puzzle**)
jigsaw puzzle

el dominó
dominoes

los dardos
darts

el comodín
joker

el joto (^C**la jota**)
jack

la reina
queen

el rey
king

el as
ace

el diamante
(^C**el rombo**)
diamond

la espada
(^C**la pica**)
spade

barajar | shuffle (v)

el corazón
heart

el trébol
club

las cartas
cards

repartir (^C**dar**) | deal (v)

vocabulario • vocabulary

el turno move	**ganar** win (v)	**el perdedor** loser	**el punto** point	**el bridge** bridge	**¿A quién le toca?** Whose turn is it?
jugar play (v)	**el ganador** winner	**la partida** game	**la puntuación** score	**la baraja** deck of cards	**Te toca a ti.** It's your move.
el jugador player	**perder** lose (v)	**la apuesta** bet	**el póquer** poker	**el palo** suit	**Tira los dados.** Roll the dice.

las manualidades 1 • arts and crafts 1

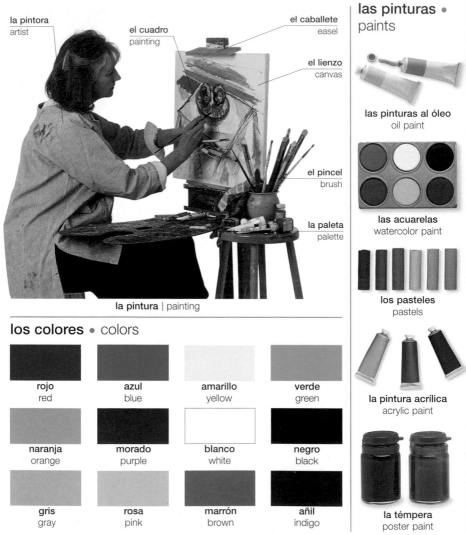

la pintora artist

el cuadro painting

el caballete easel

el lienzo canvas

el pincel brush

la paleta palette

la pintura | painting

las pinturas • paints

las pinturas al óleo oil paint

las acuarelas watercolor paint

los pasteles pastels

la pintura acrílica acrylic paint

la témpera poster paint

los colores • colors

rojo red	**azul** blue	**amarillo** yellow	**verde** green
naranja orange	**morado** purple	**blanco** white	**negro** black
gris gray	**rosa** pink	**marrón** brown	**añil** indigo

las otras manualidades • other crafts

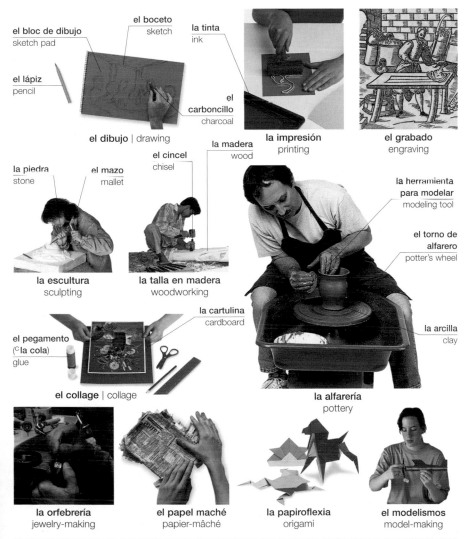

el bloc de dibujo
sketch pad

el lápiz
pencil

el boceto
sketch

la tinta
ink

el carboncillo
charcoal

el dibujo | drawing

la madera
wood

la impresión
printing

el grabado
engraving

la piedra
stone

el mazo
mallet

el cincel
chisel

la herramienta
para modelar
modeling tool

el torno de
alfarero
potter's wheel

la escultura
sculpting

la talla en madera
woodworking

la cartulina
cardboard

el pegamento
(C la cola)
glue

la arcilla
clay

el collage | collage

la alfarería
pottery

la orfebrería
jewelry-making

el papel maché
papier-mâché

la papiroflexia
origami

el modelismos
model-making

las manualidades 2 • arts and crafts 2

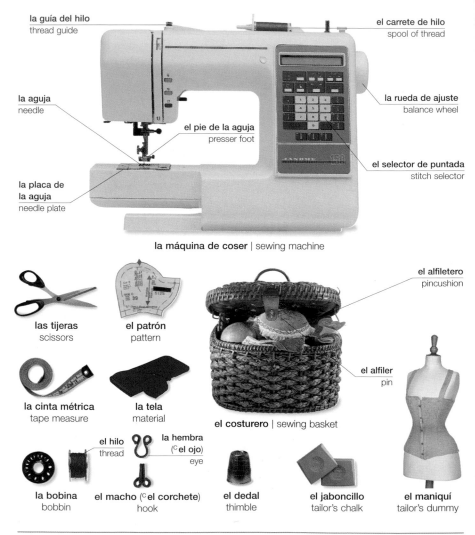

la guía del hilo | thread guide

el carrete de hilo | spool of thread

la aguja | needle

el pie de la aguja | presser foot

la rueda de ajuste | balance wheel

la placa de la aguja | needle plate

el selector de puntada | stitch selector

la máquina de coser | sewing machine

las tijeras | scissors

el patrón | pattern

el alfiletero | pincushion

el alfiler | pin

la cinta métrica | tape measure

la tela | material

el costurero | sewing basket

el hilo | thread

la hembra (ᶜel ojo) | eye

la bobina | bobbin

el macho (ᶜel corchete) | hook

el dedal | thimble

el jaboncillo | tailor's chalk

el maniquí | tailor's dummy

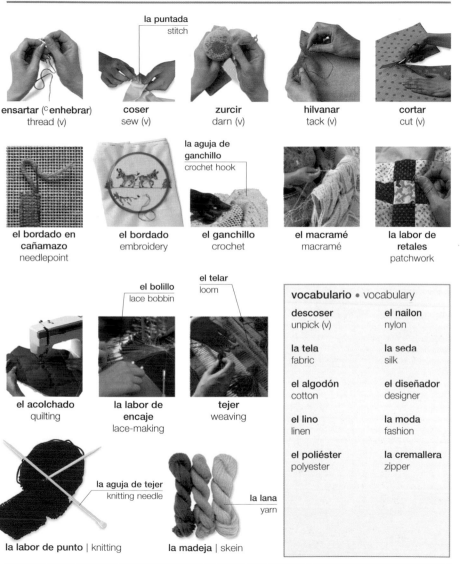

la puntada
stitch

ensartar (ᶜenhebrar)
thread (v)

coser
sew (v)

zurcir
darn (v)

hilvanar
tack (v)

cortar
cut (v)

el bordado en cañamazo
needlepoint

el bordado
embroidery

la aguja de ganchillo
crochet hook

el ganchillo
crochet

el macramé
macramé

la labor de retales
patchwork

el telar
loom

el bolillo
lace bobbin

el acolchado
quilting

la labor de encaje
lace-making

tejer
weaving

la aguja de tejer
knitting needle

la lana
yarn

la labor de punto | knitting

la madeja | skein

vocabulario • vocabulary

descoser unpick (v)	**el nailon** nylon
la tela fabric	**la seda** silk
el algodón cotton	**el diseñador** designer
el lino linen	**la moda** fashion
el poliéster polyester	**la cremallera** zipper

el medio ambiente
environment

el espacio • space

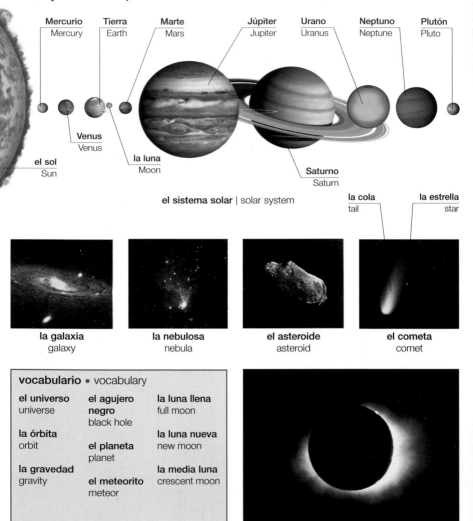

Mercurio Mercury	**Tierra** Earth	**Marte** Mars	**Júpiter** Jupiter	**Urano** Uranus	**Neptuno** Neptune	**Plutón** Pluto

Venus
Venus

la luna
Moon

el sol
Sun

Saturno
Saturn

el sistema solar | solar system

la cola
tail

la estrella
star

la galaxia
galaxy

la nebulosa
nebula

el asteroide
asteroid

el cometa
comet

vocabulario • vocabulary

el universo universe	**el agujero negro** black hole	**la luna llena** full moon
la órbita orbit	**el planeta** planet	**la luna nueva** new moon
la gravedad gravity	**el meteorito** meteor	**la media luna** crescent moon

el eclipse | eclipse

la exploración espacial • space exploration

el radar
radar

el propulsor
thruster

el transbordador
espacial
space shuttle

el
lanzacohetes
booster

la escotilla
crew hatch

el traje espacial
space suit

el **astronauta** | astronaut

el **módulo lunar** | lunar module

la rampa de lanzamiento
launch pad

el lanzamiento
launch

el satélite
satellite

la estación espacial
space station

la astronomía • astronomy

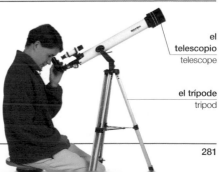

la constelación
constellation

los prismáticos
binoculars

el
telescopio
telescope

el trípode
tripod

la Tierra • Earth

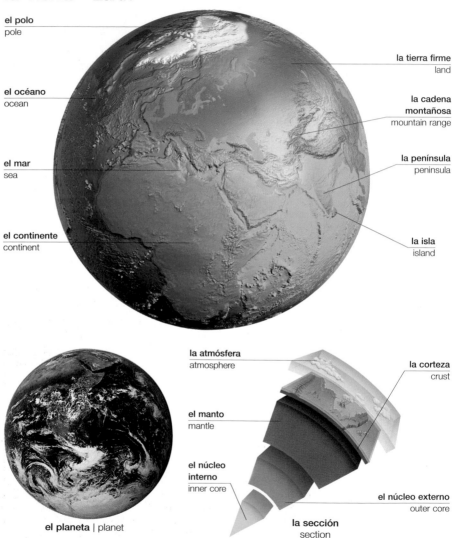

el polo
pole

el océano
ocean

el mar
sea

el continente
continent

la tierra firme
land

la cadena montañosa
mountain range

la península
peninsula

la isla
island

la atmósfera
atmosphere

la corteza
crust

el manto
mantle

el núcleo interno
inner core

el núcleo externo
outer core

el planeta | planet

la sección
section

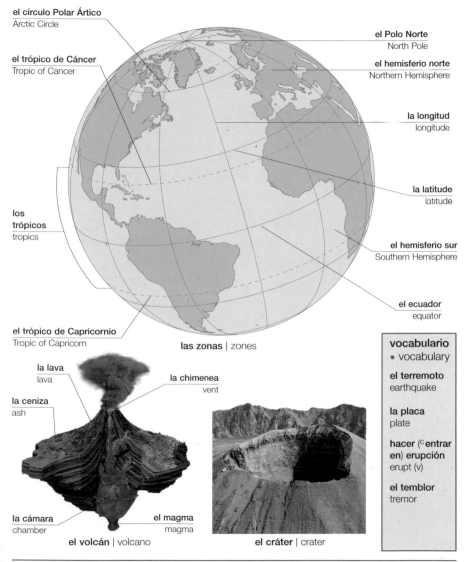

el círculo Polar Ártico
Arctic Circle

el Polo Norte
North Pole

el trópico de Cáncer
Tropic of Cancer

el hemisferio norte
Northern Hemisphere

la longitud
longitude

la latitude
latitude

los
trópicos
tropics

el hemisferio sur
Southern Hemisphere

el ecuador
equator

el trópico de Capricornio
Tropic of Capricorn

las zonas | zones

la lava
lava

la chimenea
vent

la ceniza
ash

la cámara
chamber

el magma
magma

el volcán | volcano

el cráter | crater

vocabulario
• vocabulary

el terremoto
earthquake

la placa
plate

hacer (^c **entrar
en) erupción**
erupt (v)

el temblor
tremor

el paisaje • landscape

la montaña
mountain

la ladera
slope

la orilla
bank

el río
river

los rápidos
rapids

las rocas
rocks

el glaciar
glacier

el valle | valley

la colina
hill

la meseta
plateau

el desfiladero
gorge

la cueva
cave

la llanura | plain   el desierto | desert   el bosque | forest   el bosque | woods

la selva tropical
rain forest

el pantano
swamp

el prado
meadow

la pradera
grassland

 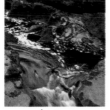  

la cascada
waterfall

el arroyo
stream

el lago
lake

el géiser
geyser

la costa
coast

el acantilado
cliff

el arrecife de coral
coral reef

el estuario
estuary

el tiempo • weather

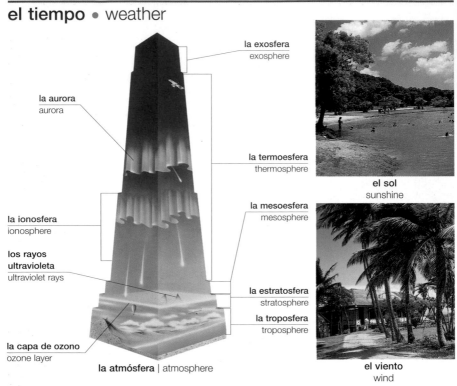

la exosfera
exosphere

la aurora
aurora

la termoesfera
thermosphere

la mesoesfera
mesosphere

la ionosfera
ionosphere

los rayos
ultravioleta
ultraviolet rays

la estratosfera
stratosphere

la troposfera
troposphere

la capa de ozono
ozone layer

la atmósfera | atmosphere

el sol
sunshine

el viento
wind

vocabulario • vocabulary

el aguanieve sleet	el chubasco shower	caluroso hot	seco dry	ventoso windy	Tengo calor/frío. I'm hot/cold.
el granizo hail	soleado sunny	frío cold	lluvioso wet	el temporal gale	Está lloviendo. It's raining.
el trueno thunder	nublado cloudy	cálido warm	húmedo humid	la température temperature	Estamos a... grados. It's... degrees.

el relámpago
lightning

la nube
cloud

la lluvia
rain

la tormenta
storm

la neblina
mist

la niebla
fog

el arcoiris
rainbow

el carámbano
icicle

la nieve
snow

la escarcha
frost

el hielo
ice

la helada
freeze

el huracán
hurricane

el tornado
tornado

el monzón
monsoon

la inundación
flood

las rocas • rocks

ígneo • igneous

el granito
granite

la obsidiana
obsidian

el basalto
basalt

la piedra pómez
pumice

sedimentario • sedimentary

la piedra arenisca
sandstone

la piedra caliza
limestone

la tiza
chalk

el pedernal
flint

el conglomerado
conglomerate

el carbón
coal

metamórfico • metamorphic

la pizarra
slate

el esquisto
schist

el gneis
gneiss

el mármol
marble

las gemas • gems

el rubí
ruby

la aguamarina
aquamarine

la amatista
amethyst

el diamante
diamond

el jade
jade

el azabache
jet

la esmeralda
emerald

el ópalo
opal

el zafiro
sapphire

la adularia
(C la piedra lunar)
moonstone

el granate
garnet

el topacio
topaz

la turmalina
tourmaline

los minerales • minerals

el cuarzo
quartz

la mica
mica

el azufre
sulfur

la hematita
(ᶜ**el hematites**)
hematite

la calcita
calcite

la malaquita
malachite

la turquesa
turquoise

el ónix (ᶜ**el ónice**)
onyx

el ágata
agate

el grafito
graphite

los metales • metals

el oro
gold

la plata
silver

el platino
platinum

el níquel
nickel

el hierro
iron

el cobre
copper

el estaño
tin

el aluminio
aluminum

el mercurio
mercury

el zinc
zinc

los animales 1 • animals 1
los mamíferos • mammals

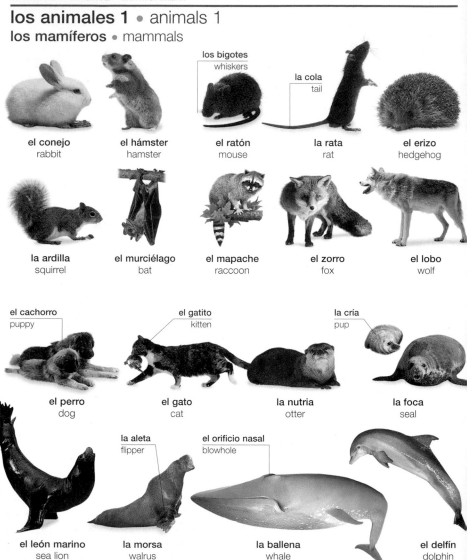

los bigotes
whiskers

la cola
tail

el conejo
rabbit

el hámster
hamster

el ratón
mouse

la rata
rat

el erizo
hedgehog

la ardilla
squirrel

el murciélago
bat

el mapache
raccoon

el zorro
fox

el lobo
wolf

el cachorro
puppy

el gatito
kitten

la cría
pup

el perro
dog

el gato
cat

la nutria
otter

la foca
seal

la aleta
flipper

el orificio nasal
blowhole

el león marino
sea lion

la morsa
walrus

la ballena
whale

el delfín
dolphin

la cornamenta
antler

la crin
mane

la joroba
(ᶜla giba)
hump

la pezuña
hoof

el ciervo
deer

la cebra
zebra

la jirafa
giraffe

el camello
camel

la trompa
trunk

el colmillo
tusk

el cuerno
horn

el hipopótamo
hippopotamus

el elefante
elephant

el rinoceronte
rhinoceros

el tigre
tiger

la melena
mane

el león
lion

el chango (ᶜel mono)
monkey

el gorila
gorilla

el koala
koala

la bolsa
pouch

el oso panda
panda

la zarpa
claw

el canguro
kangaroo

el oso
bear

el oso polar
polar bear

los animales 2 • animals 2
las aves • birds

la cola
tail

el canario
canary

el gorrión
sparrow

el colibrí
hummingbird

la golondrina
swallow

la corneja
crow

la paloma
pigeon

el pájaro carpintero
woodpecker

el halcón
falcon

la lechuza
owl

la gaviota
gull

el águila
eagle

el pelícano
pelican

el flamenco
flamingo

la cigüeña
stork

la grulla
crane

el pingüino
penguin

el avestruz
ostrich

los reptiles • reptiles

la oca | goose

el cisne
swan

el pavo real
peacock

el faisán
pheasant

el guajolote (^cel pavo)
turkey

las escamas
scales

el caimán
alligator

el lagarto
lizard

la iguana
iguana

el caparazón
shell

el galápago
turtle

la tortuga
tortoise

la serpiente
snake

el pico
beak

la pluma
feather

el ala
wing

la cacatúa
cockatoo

la garra
claw

el loro
parrot

el hocico
snout

el cocodrilo
crocodile

los animales 3 • animals 3
los anfibios • amphibians

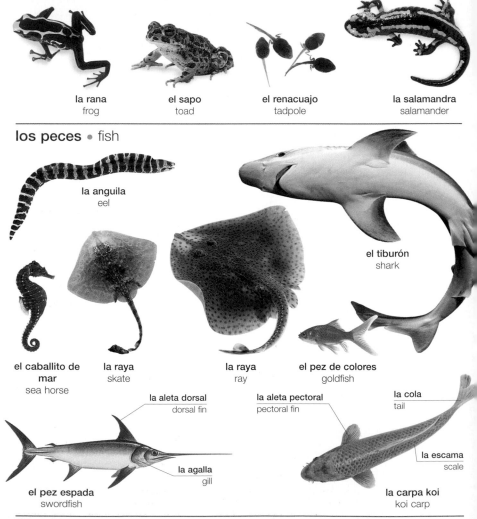

la rana
frog

el sapo
toad

el renacuajo
tadpole

la salamandra
salamander

los peces • fish

la anguila
eel

el tiburón
shark

el caballito de mar
sea horse

la raya
skate

la raya
ray

el pez de colores
goldfish

la aleta dorsal
dorsal fin

la aleta pectoral
pectoral fin

la cola
tail

la agalla
gill

la escama
scale

el pez espada
swordfish

la carpa koi
koi carp

los invertebrados • invertebrates

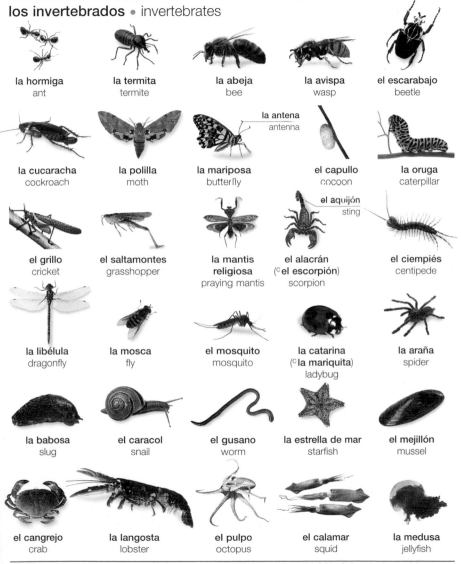

la hormiga
ant

la termita
termite

la abeja
bee

la avispa
wasp

el escarabajo
beetle

la cucaracha
cockroach

la polilla
moth

la mariposa
butterfly

la antena
antenna

el capullo
cocoon

la oruga
caterpillar

el grillo
cricket

el saltamontes
grasshopper

la mantis religiosa
praying mantis

el aguijón
sting

el alacrán
(ᶜel escorpión)
scorpion

el ciempiés
centipede

la libélula
dragonfly

la mosca
fly

el mosquito
mosquito

la catarina
(ᶜla mariquita)
ladybug

la araña
spider

la babosa
slug

el caracol
snail

el gusano
worm

la estrella de mar
starfish

el mejillón
mussel

el cangrejo
crab

la langosta
lobster

el pulpo
octopus

el calamar
squid

la medusa
jellyfish

las plantas • plants

el árbol • tree

la rama
branch

la hoja
leaf

la ramita
twig

la corteza
bark

el sauce
willow

la raíz
root

el tronco
trunk

el roble
oak

el álamo
poplar

el eucalipto
eucalyptus

el alerce
larch

la haya
beech

el abedul
birch

el pino
pine

el cedro
cedar

el arce
maple

el olmo
elm

el tilo
lime

el acebo
holly

la baya
berry

la palmera
palm

la planta de flor • flowering plant

la flor
flower

el estambre
stamen

el pétalo
petal

el cáliz
calyx

el tallo
stalk

el tallo
stem

el capullo
bud

el ranúnculo
buttercup

la margarita
daisy

el cardo
thistle

el diente de león
dandelion

el brezo
heather

la amapola
poppy

la dedalera
foxglove

la madreselva
honeysuckle

el girasol
sunflower

el trébol
clover

los narcisos
silvestres
bluebells

la prímula
primrose

los lupinos
lupines

la ortiga
nettle

la ciudad • town

la calle
street

el borde de la
banqueta (^C el bordillo)
curb

la esquina
street corner

la tienda
store

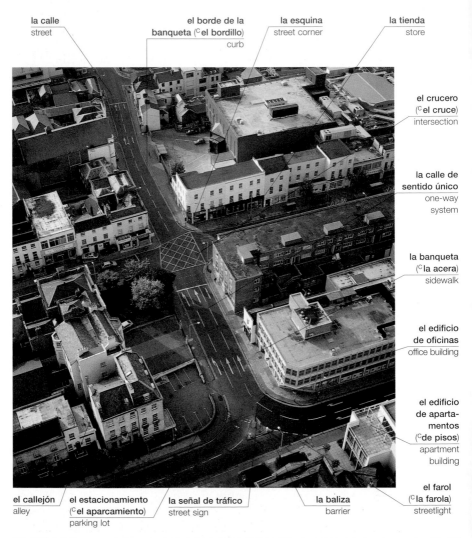

el crucero
(^C el cruce)
intersection

la calle de
sentido único
one-way
system

la banqueta
(^C la acera)
sidewalk

el edificio
de oficinas
office building

el edificio
de aparta-
mentos
(^Cde pisos)
apartment
building

el farol
(^C la farola)
streetlight

el callejón
alley

el estacionamiento
(^Cel aparcamiento)
parking lot

la señal de tráfico
street sign

la baliza
barrier

los edificios • buildings

el palacio municipal
town hall

la biblioteca
library

el cine
movie theater

el teatro
theater

la universidad
university

el rascacielos
skyscraper

la escuela
school

las zonas • areas

la zona industrial
industrial park

la ciudad
city

el suburbio
(ᶜ **la periferia**)
suburb

el pueblo
village

---

vocabulario • vocabulary

la zona peatonal pedestrian zone	**la calle lateral** side street	**la parada de autobús** bus stop	**la alcantarilla** gutter	**la iglesia** church
la avenida avenue	**la plaza** square	**la coladera** (ᶜ **la boca de alcantarilla**) manhole	**la fábrica** factory	**el drenaje** (ᶜ **el sumidero**) drain

---

la arquitectura • architecture

los edificios y las estructuras • buildings and structures

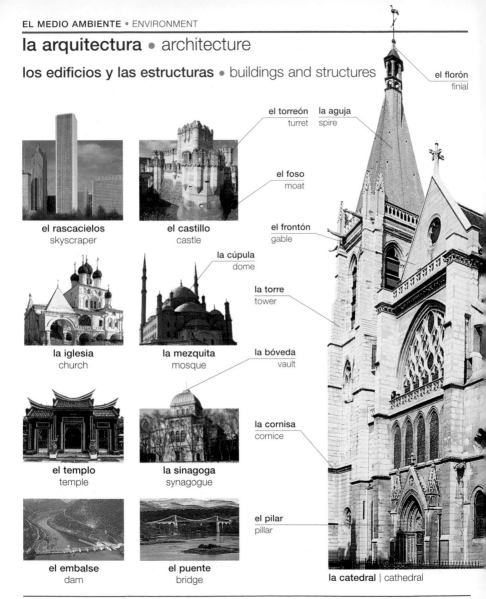

el florón
finial

el torreón
turret

la aguja
spire

el foso
moat

el rascacielos
skyscraper

el castillo
castle

el frontón
gable

la cúpula
dome

la torre
tower

la iglesia
church

la mezquita
mosque

la bóveda
vault

la cornisa
cornice

el templo
temple

la sinagoga
synagogue

el pilar
pillar

el embalse
dam

el puente
bridge

la catedral | cathedral

los estilos • styles

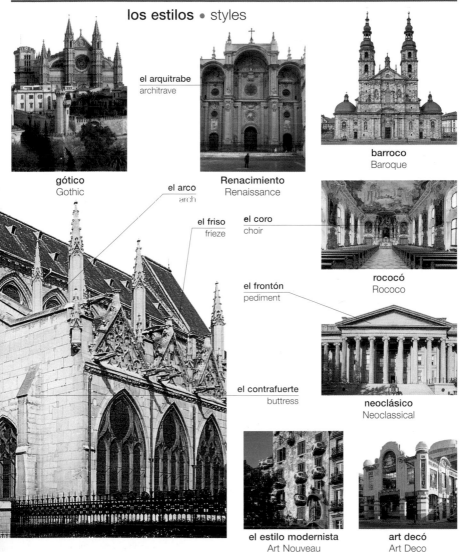

el arquitrabe
architrave

barroco
Baroque

gótico
Gothic

el arco
arch

Renacimiento
Renaissance

el friso
frieze

el coro
choir

rococó
Rococo

el frontón
pediment

el contrafuerte
buttress

neoclásico
Neoclassical

el estilo modernista
Art Nouveau

art decó
Art Deco

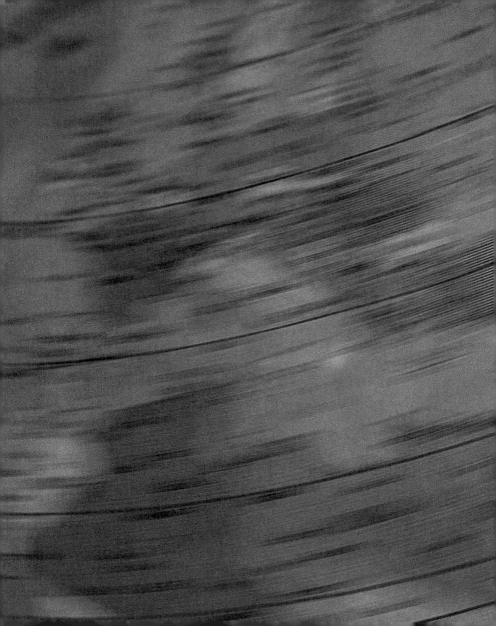

los datos
reference

el tiempo • time

el minutero
minute hand

la manecilla (ᶜla aguja) de la hora
hour hand

el reloj
clock

vocabulario • vocabulary

el segundo second	**ahora** now	**un cuarto de hora** a quarter of an hour
el minuto minute	**más tarde** later	**veinte minutos** twenty minutes
la hora hour	**media hora** half an hour	**cuarenta minutos** forty minutes

¿Qué hora es?
What time is it?

Son las tres en punto.
It's three o'clock.

la una y cinco
five past one

la una y diez
ten past one

la una y cuarto
quarter past one

la una y veinte
twenty past one

el segundero
second hand

la una y veinticinco
twenty-five past one

la una y media
one thirty

las veinticinco para las dos (ᶜlas dos menos veinticinco)
twenty-five to two

las veinte para las dos (ᶜlas dos menos veinte)
twenty to two

el cuarto para las dos (ᶜlas dos menos cuarto)
quarter to two

las diez para las dos (ᶜlas dos menos diez)
ten to two

las cinco para las dos (ᶜlas dos menos cinco)
five to two

las dos en punto
two o'clock

la noche y el día • night and day

la medianoche
midnight

el amanecer
sunrise

el alba
dawn

la mañana
morning

el atardecer
(ᶜ**la puesta de sol**)
sunset

el mediodía
noon

el anochecer
dusk

la noche
evening

la tarde
afternoon

vocabulario • vocabulary

temprano early	**Llegas temprano.** You're early.	**Por favor, sé puntual.** Please be on time.	**¿A qué hora termina?** What time does it end?
puntual on time	**Llegas tarde.** You're late.	**Hasta luego.** I'll see you later.	**¿Cuánto dura?** How long will it last?
tarde late	**Llegaré dentro de poco.** I'll be there soon.	**¿A qué hora comienza?** What time does it start?	**Se está haciendo tarde.** It's getting late.

el calendario • calendar

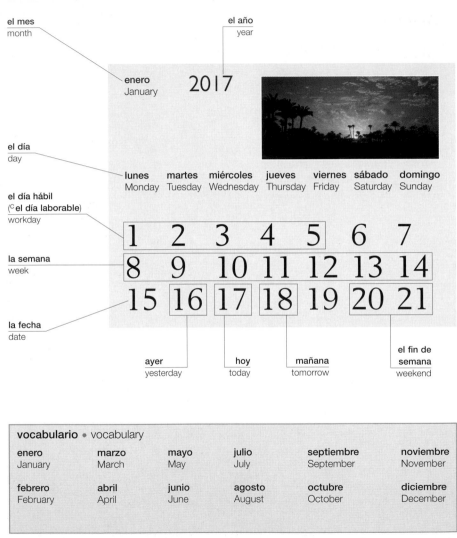

el mes
month

el año
year

enero
January

2017

el día
day

lunes	**martes**	**miércoles**	**jueves**	**viernes**	**sábado**	**domingo**
Monday	Tuesday	Wednesday	Thursday	Friday	Saturday	Sunday

el día hábil
(^C**el día laborable**)
workday

la semana
week

la fecha
date

1	2	3	4	5	6	7
8	9	10	11	12	13	14
15	16	17	18	19	20	21

ayer
yesterday

hoy
today

mañana
tomorrow

el fin de semana
weekend

---

vocabulario • vocabulary

enero January	**marzo** March	**mayo** May	**julio** July	**septiembre** September	**noviembre** November
febrero February	**abril** April	**junio** June	**agosto** August	**octubre** October	**diciembre** December

---

los años • years

1900	**mil novecientos** • nineteen hundred
1901	**mil novecientos uno** • nineteen hundred and one
1910	**mil novecientos diez** • nineteen ten
2000	**dos mil** • two thousand
2001	**dos mil uno** • two thousand and one

las estaciones • seasons

la primavera
spring

el verano
summer

el otoño
fall

el invierno
winter

---

vocabulario • vocabulary

el siglo century	**la semana pasada** last week	**mensual** monthly
la década decade	**la semana que viene** next week	**anual** annual
el milenio millennium	**anteayer** (ᶜantes de ayer) the day before yesterday	
quince días two weeks	**pasado mañana** the day after tomorrow	**¿Qué día es hoy?** What's the date today?
esta semana this week	**semanalmente** weekly	**Es el siete de febrero de dos mil diecisiete.** It's February seventh, two thousand and seventeen.

---

los números • numbers

0	**cero** • zero		20	**veinte** • twenty
1	**uno** • one		21	**veintiuno** • twenty-one
2	**dos** • two		22	**veintidós** • twenty-two
3	**tres** • three		30	**treinta** • thirty
4	**cuatro** • four		40	**cuarenta** • forty
5	**cinco** • five		50	**cincuenta** • fifty
6	**seis** • six		60	**sesenta** • sixty
7	**siete** • seven		70	**setenta** • seventy
8	**ocho** • eight		80	**ochenta** • eighty
9	**nueve** • nine		90	**noventa** • ninety
10	**diez** • ten		100	**cien** • one hundred
11	**once** • eleven		110	**ciento diez** • one hundred and ten
12	**doce** • twelve		200	**doscientos** • two hundred
13	**trece** • thirteen		300	**trescientos** • three hundred
14	**catorce** • fourteen		400	**cuatrocientos** • four hundred
15	**quince** • fifteen		500	**quinientos** • five hundred
16	**dieciséis** • sixteen		600	**seiscientos** • six hundred
17	**diecisiete** • seventeen		700	**setecientos** • seven hundred
18	**dieciocho** • eighteen		800	**ochocientos** • eight hundred
19	**diecinueve** • nineteen		900	**novecientos** • nine hundred

1,000   **mil** • one thousand

10,000   **diez mil** • ten thousand

20,000   **veinte mil** • twenty thousand

50,000   **cincuenta mil** • fifty thousand

55,500   **cincuenta y cinco mil quinientos** • fifty-five thousand five hundred

100,000   **cien mil** • one hundred thousand

1,000,000   **un millón** • one million

1,000,000,000   **mil millones** • one billion

primero
first

segundo
second

tercero
third

cuarto • fourth

quinto • fifth

sexto • sixth

séptimo • seventh

octavo • eighth

noveno • ninth

décimo • tenth

undécimo • eleventh

duodécimo • twelfth

decimotercero • thirteenth

decimocuarto • fourteenth

decimoquinto • fifteenth

decimosexto
• sixteenth

decimoséptimo
• seventeenth

décimo octavo
• eighteenth

décimo noveno
• nineteenth

vigésimo • twentieth

vigésimo primero
• twenty-first

vigésimo segundo
• twenty-second

vigésimo tercero
• twenty-third

trigésimo • thirtieth

cuadragésimo
• fortieth

quincuagésimo
• fiftieth

sexagésimo • sixtieth

septuagésimo
• seventieth

octogésimo
• eightieth

nonagésimo
• ninetieth

centésimo
• (one) hundredth

los pesos y las medidas • weights and measures

el área • area

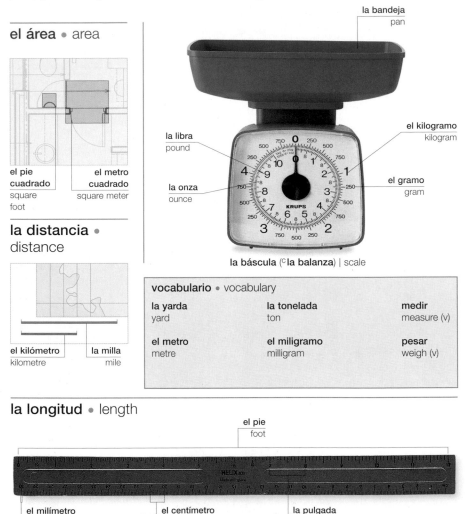

el pie cuadrado
square foot

el metro cuadrado
square meter

la distancia • distance

el kilómetro
kilometre

la milla
mile

la bandeja
pan

la libra
pound

la onza
ounce

el kilogramo
kilogram

el gramo
gram

la báscula (^C**la balanza**) | scale

vocabulario • vocabulary

la yarda yard	**la tonelada** ton	**medir** measure (v)
el metro metre	**el miligramo** milligram	**pesar** weigh (v)

la longitud • length

el pie
foot

el milímetro
millimeter

el centímetro
centimeter

la pulgada
inch

la capacidad • capacity

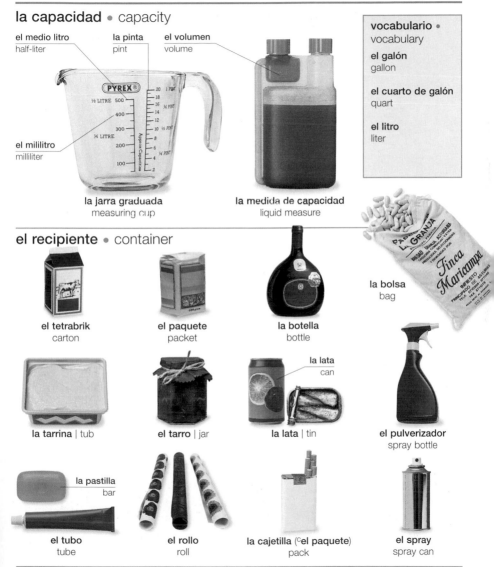

el medio litro
half-liter

la pinta
pint

el volumen
volume

PYREX®

el mililitro
milliliter

la jarra graduada
measuring cup

la medida de capacidad
liquid measure

el recipiente • container

el tetrabrik
carton

el paquete
packet

la botella
bottle

la bolsa
bag

la tarrina | tub

el tarro | jar

la lata
can

la lata | tin

el pulverizador
spray bottle

la pastilla
bar

el tubo
tube

el rollo
roll

la cajetilla (ᶜel paquete)
pack

el spray
spray can

el mapamundi • world map

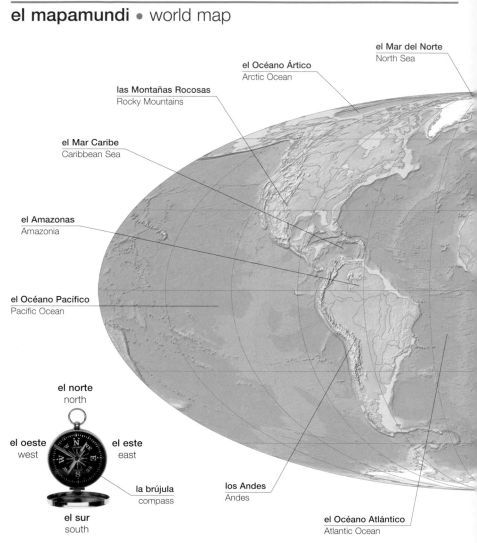

el Mar del Norte
North Sea

el Océano Ártico
Arctic Ocean

las Montañas Rocosas
Rocky Mountains

el Mar Caribe
Caribbean Sea

el Amazonas
Amazonia

el Océano Pacífico
Pacific Ocean

el norte
north

el oeste
west

el este
east

la brújula
compass

los Andes
Andes

el Océano Atlántico
Atlantic Ocean

el sur
south

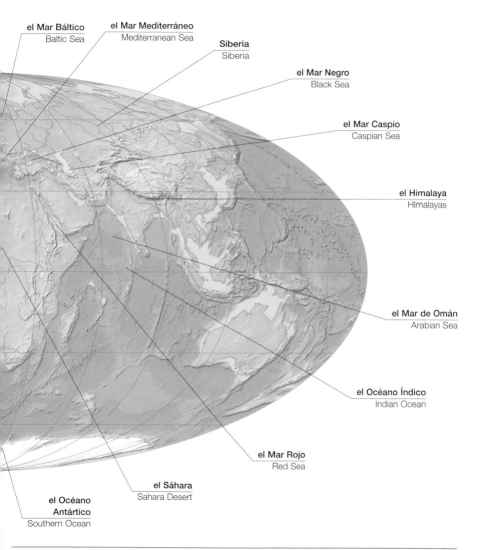

el Mar Báltico
Baltic Sea

el Mar Mediterráneo
Mediterranean Sea

Siberia
Siberia

el Mar Negro
Black Sea

el Mar Caspio
Caspian Sea

el Himalaya
Himalayas

el Mar de Omán
Arabian Sea

el Océano Índico
Indian Ocean

el Mar Rojo
Red Sea

el Sáhara
Sahara Desert

el Océano
Antártico
Southern Ocean

América del Norte y Central • North and Central America

Hawaii
Hawaii

1 **Alaska** • Alaska
2 **Canadá** • Canada
3 **Groenlandia** • Greenland
4 **Estados Unidos de América** •
United States of America
5 **México** • Mexico
6 **Guatemala** • Guatemala
7 **Belice** • Belize
8 **El Salvador** • El Salvador
9 **Honduras** • Honduras
10 **Nicaragua** • Nicaragua
11 **Costa Rica** • Costa Rica
12 **Panamá** • Panama
13 **Cuba** • Cuba
14 **Bahamas** • Bahamas
15 **Jamaica** • Jamaica
16 **Haití** • Haiti
17 **República Dominicana** •
Dominican Republic
18 **Puerto Rico** • Puerto Rico
19 **Barbados** • Barbados
20 **Trinidad y Tobago** • Trinidad and Tobago
21 **Saint Kitts y Nevis** • St. Kitts and Nevis

22 **Antigua y Barbuda** • Antigua and Barbuda
23 **Dominica** • Dominica
24 **Santa Lucía** • St. Lucia
25 **San Vicente y las Granadinas** •
St. Vincent and the Grenadines
26 **Granada** • Grenada

América del Sur • South America

1 **Venezuela** • Venezuela

2 **Colombia** • Colombia

3 **Ecuador** • Ecuador

4 **Perú** • Peru

5 **las Islas Galápagos** •
  Galápagos Islands

6 **Guyana** • Guyana

7 **Suriname** • Suriname

8 **la Guayana Francesa** •
  French Guiana

9 **Brasil** • Brazil

10 **Bolivia** • Bolivia

11 **Chile** • Chile

12 **Argentina** • Argentina

13 **Paraguay** • Paraguay

14 **Uruguay** • Uruguay

15 **las Malvinas** •
  Falkland Islands

vocabulario • vocabulary

el continente	el principado	la provincia
continent	principality	province
el país	**el territorio**	**el distrito**
country	territory	district
la nación	**la colonia**	**la región**
nation	colony	region
el estado	**la zona**	**la capital**
state	zone	capital

Europa • Europe

1 **Irlanda** • Ireland
2 **Reino Unido** • United Kingdom
3 **Portugal** • Portugal
4 **España** • Spain
5 **las Islas Baleares** • Balearic Islands
6 **Andorra** • Andorra
7 **Francia** • France
8 **Bélgica** • Belgium
9 **los Países Bajos** • Netherlands
10 **Luxemburgo** • Luxembourg
11 **Alemania** • Germany
12 **Dinamarca** • Denmark
13 **Noruega** • Norway
14 **Suecia** • Sweden
15 **Finlandia** • Finland
16 **Estonia** • Estonia
17 **Letonia** • Latvia
18 **Lituania** • Lithuania
19 **Kaliningrado** • Kaliningrad
20 **Polonia** • Poland
21 **República Checa** • Czech Republic
22 **Austria** • Austria
23 **Liechtenstein** • Liechtenstein
24 **Suiza** • Switzerland
25 **Italia** • Italy
26 **Mónaco** • Monaco
27 **Córcega** • Corsica
28 **Cerdeña** • Sardinia
29 **San Marino** • San Marino

30 **la Ciudad del Vaticano** • Vatican City
31 **Sicilia** • Sicily
32 **Malta** • Malta
33 **Eslovenia** • Slovenia
34 **Croacia** • Croatia
35 **Hungría** • Hungary
36 **Eslovaquia** • Slovakia
37 **Ucrania** • Ukraine
38 **Belarús** • Belarus
39 **Moldavia** • Moldova

40 **Rumanía** • Romania
41 **Serbia** • Serbia
42 **Bosnia y Herzegovina** • Bosnia and Herzegovina
43 **Albania** • Albania
44 **Macedonia** • Macedonia
45 **Bulgaria** • Bulgaria
46 **Grecia** • Greece
47 **Kosovo** • Kosovo
48 **Montenegro** • Montenegro
49 **Islandia** • Iceland

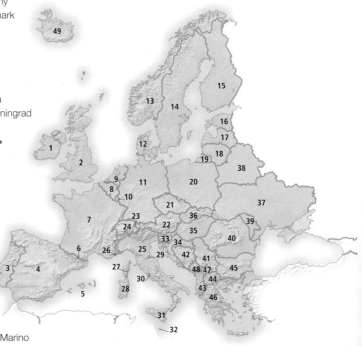

África • Africa

1 **Marruecos** • Morocco
2 **Sáhara Occidental** •
  Western Sahara
3 **Mauritania** •
  Mauritania
4 **Senegal** • Senegal
5 **Gambia** • Gambia
6 **Guinea-Bissau** •
  Guinea-Bissau
7 **Guinea** • Guinea
8 **Sierra Leona** •
  Sierra Leone
9 **Liberia** • Liberia
10 **Costa de Marfil** •
  Ivory Coast
11 **Burquina Faso** •
  Burkina Faso
12 **Malí** • Mali
13 **Argelia** • Algeria
14 **Túnez** • Tunisia
15 **Libia** • Libya
16 **Níger** • Niger
17 **Ghana** • Ghana
18 **Togo** • Togo

19 **Benin** • Benin
20 **Nigeria** • Nigeria
21 **Santo Tomé y Príncipe** •
  São Tomé and Principe
22 **Guinea Ecuatorial** •
  Equatorial Guinea
23 **Camerún** • Cameroon
24 **Chad** • Chad
25 **Egipto** • Egypt
26 **Sudán** • Sudan
27 **Sudán del Sur** • South Sudan
28 **Eritrea** • Eritrea
29 **Djibouti** • Djibouti
30 **Etiopía** • Ethiopia
31 **Somalia** • Somalia

32 **Kenya** • Kenya
33 **Uganda** • Uganda
34 **República Centroafricana** •
  Central African Republic
35 **Gabón** • Gabon
36 **Congo** • Congo
37 **Cabinda** • Cabinda
38 **República Democrática del
  Congo** • Democratic
  Republic of the Congo
39 **Rwanda** • Rwanda
40 **Burundi** • Burundi
41 **Tanzania** • Tanzania
42 **Mozambique** •
  Mozambique
43 **Malawi** • Malawi
44 **Zambia** • Zambia
45 **Angola** • Angola
46 **Namibia** • Namibia
47 **Botswana** • Botswana
48 **Zimbabwe** • Zimbabwe
49 **Sudáfrica** • South Africa
50 **Lesotho** • Lesotho
51 **Swazilandia** • Swaziland
52 **Comoros** • Comoros
53 **Madagascar** • Madagascar
54 **Mauricio** • Mauritius

Asia • Asia

1 **la Turchia** • Turkey

2 **Cipro** • Cyprus

3 **Federación Rusa** • Russian Federation

4 **Georgia** • Georgia

5 **Armenia** • Armenia

6 **Azerbaiyán** • Azerbaijan

7 **Irán** • Iran

8 **Iraq** • Iraq

9 **Siria** • Syria

10 **Líbano** • Lebanon

11 **Israel** • Israel

12 **Jordania** • Jordan

13 **Arabia Saudita** • Saudi Arabia

14 **Kuwait** • Kuwait

15 **Bahrein** • Bahrain

16 **Qatar** • Qatar

17 **Emiratos Árabes Unidos** • United Arab Emirates

18 **Omán** • Oman

19 **Yemen** • Yemen

20 **Kazajstán** • Kazakhstan

21 **Uzbekistán** • Uzbekistan

22 **Turkmenistán** • Turkmenistan

23 **Afganistán** • Afghanistan

24 **Tayikistán** • Tajikistan

25 **Kirguistán** • Kyrgyzstan

26 **Pakistán** • Pakistan

27 **India** • India

28 **Maldivas** • Maldives

29 **Sri Lanka** • Sri Lanka

30 **China** • China

31 **Mongolia** • Mongolia

32 **Corea del Norte** • North Korea

33 **Corea del Sur** • South Korea

34 **Japón** • Japan

35 **Nepal** • Nepal

36 **Bhutan** • Bhutan

37 **Bangladesh** • Bangladesh

38 **Myanmar (Birmania)** • Myanmar (Burma)

39 **Tailandia** • Thailand

40 **Laos** • Laos

41 **Viet Nam** • Vietnam

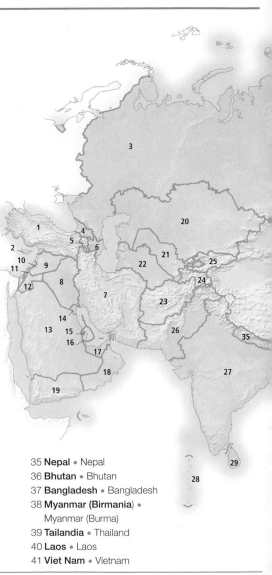

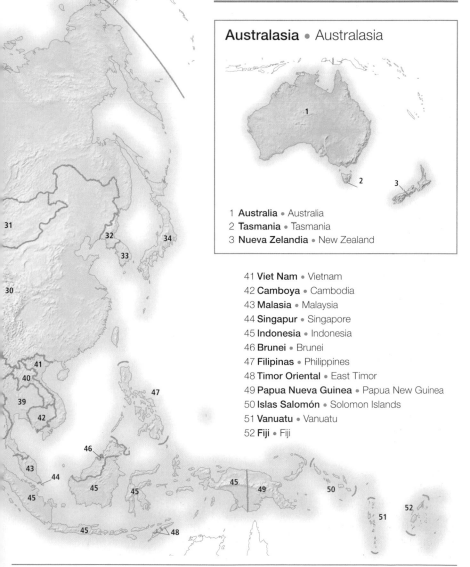

Australasia • Australasia

1 **Australia** • Australia
2 **Tasmania** • Tasmania
3 **Nueva Zelandia** • New Zealand

41 **Viet Nam** • Vietnam
42 **Camboya** • Cambodia
43 **Malasia** • Malaysia
44 **Singapur** • Singapore
45 **Indonesia** • Indonesia
46 **Brunei** • Brunei
47 **Filipinas** • Philippines
48 **Timor Oriental** • East Timor
49 **Papua Nueva Guinea** • Papua New Guinea
50 **Islas Salomón** • Solomon Islands
51 **Vanuatu** • Vanuatu
52 **Fiji** • Fiji

partículas y antónimos • particles and antonyms

a, hacia to	**de, desde** from	**para** for	**hacia** toward
encima de over	**debajo de** under	**por** along	**al otro lado** across
delante de in front of	**detrás de** behind	**con** with	**sin** without
sobre onto	**dentro de** into	**antes** before	**después** after
en in	**fuera** out	**antes de** by	**hasta** until
sobre above	**bajo** below	**temprano** early	**tarde** late
dentro inside	**fuera** outside	**ahora** now	**más tarde** later
arriba up	**abajo** down	**siempre** always	**nunca** never
en at	**más allá de** beyond	**con frecuencia** (C**a menudo**) | often	**rara vez** rarely
a través de through	**alrededor de** around	**ayer** yesterday	**mañana** tomorrow
encima de on top of	**al lado de** beside	**primer** first	**último** last
entre between	**en frente de** opposite	**cada** every	**algunos** some
cerca near	**lejos** far	**unos** about	**exactamente** exactly
aquí here	**allí** there	**un poco** a little	**mucho** a lot

grande large	**pequeño** small	**caliente** hot	**frío** cold
ancho wide	**estrecho** narrow	**abierto** open	**cerrado** closed
alto tall	**bajo** short	**lleno** full	**vacío** empty
alto high	**bajo** low	**nuevo** new	**viejo** old
grueso thick	**delgado** thin	**claro** light	**oscuro** dark
ligero light	**pesado** heavy	**fácil** easy	**difícil** difficult
duro hard	**blando** soft	**libre** free	**ocupado** occupied
húmedo wet	**seco** dry	**fuerte** strong	**débil** weak
bueno good	**malo** bad	**gordo** fat	**delgado** thin
rápido fast	**lento** slow	**joven** young	**viejo** old
correcto correct	**incorrecto** wrong	**mejor** better	**peor** worse
limpio clean	**sucio** dirty	**negro** black	**blanco** white
hermoso (C **bonito**) beautiful	**feo** ugly	**interesante** interesting	**aburrido** boring
caro expensive	**barato** cheap	**enfermo** sick	**bien** well
silencioso quiet	**ruidoso** noisy	**el principio** beginning	**el final** end

frases útiles • useful phrases

frases esenciales • essential phrases

Sí
Yes

No
No

Quizás
Maybe

Por favor
Please

Gracias
Thank you

De nada
You're welcome

Perdone
Excuse me

Lo siento
I'm sorry

No
Don't

Vale
OK

Así vale
That's fine

Está bien
That's correct

Está mal
That's wrong

saludos • greetings

Hola
Hello

Adiós
Goodbye

Buenos días
Good morning

Buenas tardes
Good afternoon

Buenas tardes
Good evening

Buenas noches
Good night

¿Cómo está?
How are you?

Me llamo…
My name is…

¿Cómo se llama?
What is your name?

¿Cómo se llama?
What is his/her name?

Le presento a…
May I introduce…

Este es…
This is…

Encantado de conocerle
Pleased to meet you

Hasta luego
See you later

letreros • signs

Información
Tourist information

Entrada
Entrance

Salida
Exit

Salida de emergencia
Emergency exit

Empuje
Push

Peligro
Danger

Prohibido fumar
No smoking

Fuera de servicio
Out of order

Horario de apertura
Opening times

Entrada libre
Free admission

Llame antes de entrar
Knock before entering

Rebajado
Reduced

Saldos
Sale

Prohibido pisar el césped
Keep off the grass

ayuda • help

¿Me puede ayudar?
Can you help me?

No entiendo
I don't understand

No lo sé
I don't know

¿Habla inglés?
Do you speak English?

Hablo inglés
I speak English

Hable más lento (ᶜdespacio), por favor
Please speak more slowly

¿Me lo puede escribir?
Please write it down for me

He perdido…
I have lost…

indicaciones •
directions

Me perdí (C**Me he perdido**) I am lost

¿Dónde está el/la…?
Where is the…?

¿Dónde está el/la… más cercano/a?
Where is the nearest…?

¿Dónde están los servicios?
Where is the restroom?

¿Cómo voy a…?
How do I get to…?

A la derecha
To the right

A la izquierda
To the left

Todo recto
Straight ahead

¿A qué distancia está…?
How far is…?

las señales de tránsito (C**las señales de tráfico**) •
road signs

Precaución I Caution

Prohibido el paso
Do not enter

Disminuir velocidad
Slow down

Desvío I Detour

Circular por la derecha
Keep right

Autopista I Freeway

Prohibido estacionar (C**Prohibido aparcar**)
No parking

Callejón sin salida
Dead end

Sentido único
One-way street

Sólo residentes
Residents only

Ceda el paso
Yield

Carretera cortada
Road closed

Obras
Roadwork

Curva peligrosa
Dangerous curve

alojamiento •
accommodation

Tengo una reservación (C**Tengo una reserva**)
I have a reservation

¿A qué hora es el desayuno?
What time is breakfast?

Volveré a las…
I'll be back at… o'clock

¿Dónde está el comedor?
Where is the dining room?

Me marcho mañana
I'm leaving tomorrow

comida y bebida •
eating and drinking

¡Salud!
Cheers!

Está buenísimo/malísimo
It's delicious/awful

Yo no bebo/fumo
I don't drink/smoke

Yo no como carne
I don't eat meat

Ya no más, gracias
No more for me, thank you

¿Puedo repetir?
May I have some more?

¿Me trae la cuenta?
May we have the check?

¿Me da un recibo?
Can I have a receipt?

Zona de fumadores
Smoking area

la salud •
health

No me encuentro bien
I don't feel well

Tengo náuseas
I feel sick

Me duele aquí
It hurts here

Tengo fiebre
I have a fever

Estoy embarrazada de… meses
I'm… months pregnant

Necesito una receta para…
I need a prescription for…

Normalmente tomo…
I normally take…

Soy alérgico a…
I'm allergic to…

¿Estará bien?
Will he/she be all right?

índice español • Spanish index

A

a 320
abadejo m 120
abajo m 120
abarrotes m 114
abdomen m 12
abdominal m 16, 251
abedul m 296
abeja f 295
abierta f 221
abierto 260, 321
abogada f 190
abogado m 180
abonar 91
abonar en la superficie 90
abono m 91
abono compuesto m 88
aborto espontáneo m 52
abrazadera f 78
abrebotellas m 68
abrelatas m 68
abrigo m 32
abril 306
absuelto 181
abuela f 22
abuelo m 22
abuelos m 23
aburrido 25, 321
acacia f 110
academia de danza f 169
acampar 266
acantilado m 285
accesorios m 36
accidente m 46
accidente de coche m 203
acciones f 77, 97, 227, 229, 233
acebo m 296
acedera f 123
aceite m 142, 199
aceite aromatizado m 134
aceite de almendras m 134
aceite de avellanas m 134
aceite de cacahuete m 135
aceite de colza m 135
aceite de girasol m 134
aceite de maíz m 135
aceite de nueces m 134
aceite de oliva m 134
aceite de presión en frío m 135
aceite de semillas de uva m 134
aceite de sésamo m 134

aceites m 134
aceites esenciales m 55
aceite vegetal m 135
aceituna negra f 143
aceituna rellena f 143
aceitunas f 151
aceituna verde f 143
acelerador m 200, 204
acelga f 123
acelga china f 123
ace m 230
acero inoxidable m 79
aclarar 76
a cobro revertido 99
acolchado m 277
acomodador m 255
acompañamiento m 153
acontecimientos de una vida m 26
acostarse 71
acotamiento m 194
actividades f 162
actividades al aire libre f 262
actor m 254
actores m 179
actriz f 191, 254
acuarelas f 274
acupresión f 55
acupuntura f 55
acusación f 180
acusado m 180, 181
aderezo m 158
adiós 322
adobado 159
adolescente f 23
adornos para el jardín m 84
adosado por un lado 58
aduana f 212
aduanas del puerto f 216
adularia f 288
adulto m 23
adversario m 236
aerodeslizador m 215
aeropuerto m 212
afeitado m 73
Afganistán 318
afilador m 68, 118
África 317
aftershave m 73
agalla f 294
agarre m 237
ágata m 289
agencia de viajes f 114
agencia inmobiliaria f 115
agenda f 173, 175
agente de bolsa m 97
agente de policia m 94
agente de viajes f 190
agente immobiliaria f 189

agitador m 150
aglomerado m 79
agosto 306
agresión f 94
agricultor m 189
agua m 144, 238
agua de colonia m 41
agua de la llave m 144
agua embotellada m 144
agua mineral m 144
aguacate m 128
aguamarina f 288
aguanieve m 286
aguarrás m 83
águila m 292
aguja f 109, 276, 300
aguja de ganchillo f 277
aguja de tejer f 277
agujero negro m 280
ahogarse 47, 239
ahora 304, 320
ahorros m 96
ahumado 118, 121, 143, 159
aikido m 236
aire acondicionado m 200
airear 91
aislamiento m 61
ajedrez m 272
ajo m 125, 132
ala m 119, 210, 293
a la carta 152
alacrán m 295
ala delta m 248
alambre m 79, 89, 155
álamo m 296
a la plancha 159
alargador m 78
alarma antirrobo f 58
alarma contra incendios f 95
Alaska 314
alba m 305
albahaca f 133
Albania 316
albañil m 186, 188
alberca f 238, 250
alberca de plástico f 263
albóndigas f 158
albornoz m 73
álbum de fotos m 271
alcachofa f 89, 124
alcachofa de la ducha m 72
alcantarilla f 299
alcaparras f 143
alcázar m 214
alcorza f 141
aldaba f 59

Alemania 316
alerce m 296
alergia f 44
alero m 58
alerón m 210
aleta f 210, 239, 290
aleta dorsal f 294
aleta pectoral f 294
aletas de raya f 120
alfalfa f 184
alfarería f 275
alfil m 272
alfiler m 276
alfiler de corbata m 36
alfiletero m 276
alfombra f 63
alfombrilla de baño f 72
algodón m 184, 277
algunos 320
alhelí m 110
al horno 159
alicatar 82
alicates m 80
alimentar 183
alimentos m 118
alimentos embotellados m 134
alisar 39, 79
al lado de 320
allí 320
almeja f 121
almendra f 122, 129
almendras f 151
almohada f 70
almohadilla f 15
al otro lado 320
alquilar 58
alquiler m 58
alrededor de 320
alta definición 269
altavoz m 209
alternador m 203
altitud f 211
alto 321
altura f 165
aluminio m 289
alumno m 162
al vapor 159
amamantar 53
amanecer m 305
amapola f 297
amargo 124, 127
amarillo 274
amarrar 217
amasar 138
amatista f 288
Amazonas m 312
ambulancero m 94
ambulancia f 94
América del Norte y Central 314
América del Sur 315
americana sport f 33

amigo m 24
amigo por correspondencia m 24
amniocentesis f 52
amperio m 60
ampliación f 58, 271
ampliar 172
amplificador m 268
ampolla f 46
nuez de la India m 129
analgésico m 109
analgésicos m 47
análisis m 49
análisis de sangre f 48
analógico 179
ancho 321
anchura f 165
ancla m 214, 240
anclar 217
andamio m 186
andar en bicicleta 207
andar en patineta 249
andén m 208
Andes m 312
Andorra 316
anestesista m 48
anfibios m 294
anfitriona f 64
anfitrión f 64
Angola 317
anguila f 294
ángulo m 164
añil 274
anillas f 89
anillo m 36
anillo cervical m 21
animales m 290, 292, 294
anís estrellado m 133
aniversario m 26
anochecer m 305
año m 306
Año Nuevo m 27
años m 307
anteayer 307
antebrazo m 12
antecedentes m 181
antena f 295
antena de radio f 214
antena parabólica f 269
antes 320
antes de 320
antiadherente 69
antiarrugas 41
anticongelante m 199
Antigua y Barbuda 314
antiinflamatorio m 109
antónimos 320
anual 86, 307
anular m 15
anuncio m 269
anzuelo m 244

español

español

español

español

español

español

español

español

español

español

español

español

índice inglés • English index

english

A

abdomen 12
abdominals 16
about 320
above 320
acacia 110
accelerator 200
accessories 36, 38
access road 216
accident 46
accountant 97, 190
accounting department 175
account number 96
accused 180
ace 230, 273
Achilles tendon 16
acorn squash 125
acquaintance 24
acquitted 181
across 320
acrylic paint 274
activities 77, 162, 245, 263
actor 254
actors 179
actress 191, 254
acupressure 55
acupuncture 55
Adam's apple 19
add v 165
addition 58
address 98
adhesive bandage 47
adhesive tape 47
adjustable wrench 80
admissions office 168
admitted 48
adult 23
advantage 230
adventure movie 255
advertisement 269
adzuki beans 131
aerate v 91
Afghanistan 318
Africa 317
after 320
afternoon 305
aftershave 73
aftersun lotion 108
agate 289
agenda 174
aikido 236
aileron 210
air bag 201
air-conditioning 200
aircraft 210
aircraft carrier 215
air cylinder 239

air filter 202, 204
airliner 210, 212
air mattress 267
airport 212
air vent 210
aisle 106, 168, 210, 254
à la carte 152
alarm clock 70
Alaska 314
Albania 316
alcoholic drinks 145
alfalfa 184
Algeria 317
Allen wrench 80
allergy 44
alley 298
alligator 293
alligator clip 167
all meals included 101
all-purpose flour 139
allspice 132
almond 129
almond oil 134
almonds 151
along 320
alpine 87
alpine skiing 247
alternating current 60
alternative therapy 54
alternator 203
altitude 211
aluminium 289
always 320
Amazonia 312
ambulance 94
amethyst 288
amniocentesis 52
amniotic fluid 52
amount 96
amp 60
amphibians 294
amplifier 268
analog 179
anchor 191, 192, 214, 240
Andes 312
Andorra 316
anesthetist 48
angle 164
angler 244
Angola 317
angry 25
animals 290, 292, 294
animated movie 255
ankle 13, 15
ankle length 34
anniversary 26
annual 86, 307
answer 163

answer v 99, 163
answering machine 99
ant 295
antenna 295
antifreeze 199
Antigua and Barbuda 314
anti-inflammatory 109
antique store 114
antiseptic 47
antiseptic wipe 47
antiwrinkle 41
antler 291
apartment 59
apartment building 59, 298
apéritif 153
aperture dial 270
apex 164
app 99
appeal 181
appearance 30
appendix 18
appetizer 153
applaud v 255
apple 126
apple corer 68
apple juice 149
appliances 66
application 176
appointment 45, 175
apricot 126
April 306
apron 30, 50, 69, 212
aquamarine 288
Arabian Sea 313
arbor 84
arborio rice 130
arc 164
arch 15, 85, 301
archery 249
architect 190
architecture 300
architrave 301
Arctic Circle 283
Arctic Ocean 312
area 165, 310
areas 299
arena 243
Argentina 315
arithmetic 165
arm 13
armchair 63
Armenia 318
armpit 13
armrest 200, 210
aromatherapy 55
around 320
arrest 94
arrivals 213

arrow 249
art 162
Art Deco 301
artery 19
art history 169
art gallery 261
artichoke 124
artist 274
Art Nouveau 301
arts and crafts 274, 276
art school 169
art supply store 115
arugula 123
ash 283
ashtray 150
Asia 318
asparagus 124
asphalt 187
assault 94
assistant 24
assisted delivery 53
asteroid 280
asthma 44
astigmatism 51
astronaut 281
astronomy 281
asymmetric bars 235
at 320
athlete 234
athletic shoes 31
Atlantic Ocean 312
ATM 97
atmosphere 282, 286
atrium 104
attachment 177
attack 220
attack zone 224
attend v 174
attic 58
attractions 261
auburn 39
audience 254
August 306
aunt 22
aurora 286
Australia 319
Austria 316
automatic 200
automatic door 196
automatic payment 96
auto racing 249
avalanche 247
avenue 299
avocado 128
awning 148
ax 95
axle 205
ayurveda 55
Azerbaijan 318

B

baby 23, 30
baby bath 74
baby care 74
baby carriage 75
baby changing room 104
baby monitor 75
baby products 107
baby sling 75
back 13, 64
backboard 226
back brush 73
backdrop 254
backgammon 272
backhand 231
backpack 31, 37, 267
backseat 200
backsplash 66
backstroke 239
backswing 233
bacon 118, 157
bacon strip 119
bad 321
badge 94, 189
badminton 231
bag 311
bag cart 233
bags 37
bagel 139
baggage carousel 212
baggage claim 213
baggage trailer 212
baguette 138
Bahamas 314
Bahrain 318
bail 181
bailiff 180
bait 244
bait v 245
bake v 67, 138
baked 159
baker 139
bakery 107, 114, 138
baking 69
balance wheel 276
balcony 59, 254
balcony seats 254
bald 39
bale 184
Balearic Islands 316
ball 15, 75, 221, 224, 226, 228, 230
ball boy 231
ballet 255
balsamic vinegar 135
Baltic Sea 313
bamboo 86, 122
banana 128

english

english

english

english

english

english

english

english

english

english

english

agradecimientos • acknowledgments

DORLING KINDERSLEY would like to thank Sanjay Chauhan, Jomin Johny, Christine Lacey, Mahua Mandal, Tracey Miles, and Sonakshi Singh for design assistance, Georgina Garner for editorial and administrative help, Polly Boyd, Sonia Gavira, Nandini Gupta, Tina Jindal, Nishtha Kapil, Smita Mathur, Antara Moitra, Cathy Meeus, Isha Sharma, Nisha Shaw, and Janashree Singha for editorial help, Claire Bowers for compiling the DK picture credits, Nishwan Rasool for picture research, and Suruchi Bhatia, Maasoom Dhillon, and William Jones for app development and creation.

The publisher would like to thank the following for their kind permission to reproduce their photographs:

Abbreviations key: a-above; b-below/bottom; c-center; f-far; l-left; r-right; t-top)

123RF.com: Andriy Popov 34tl; Brad Wynnyk 172bc; Daniel Ernst 179tc; Hongqi Zhang 24cla. 175cr; Ingvar Bjork 60c; Kobby Dagan 259c; leonardo255 269c; Liubov Vadimovna (Luba) Nel 39cla; Ljupco Smokovski 75crb; Oleksandr Marynchenko 60bl; Olga Popova 33c; oneblink 49bc; Robert Churchill 94c; Roman Gorielov 33bc; Ruslan Kudrin 35bc, 35br; Subbotina 39cra; Sutichak Yachaingkham 39tc; Tarzhanova 37tc; Vitaly Valua 39tl; Wavebreak Media Ltd 188bl; Wilawan Khasawong 75cb; **Action Plus:** 224bc; **Alamy Images:** 154t; A.T. Willett 287bcl; Alex Segre 105ca, 195cl; Ambrophoto 24cra; Blend Images 168cr; Cultura RM 33r; Doug Houghton 107fbr; Hugh Threlfall 35tl; 176tr; Ian Allenden 48br; Ian Dagnall 270t; Ievgen Chepil 250bc; imagebroker 199tl, 249c; keith morris 178c; Martyn Evans 210b; MBI 175tl; Michael Burrell 213cra; Michael Foyle 184bl; Oleksiy Maksymenko 169tr; Paul Weston 168br; Prisma Bildagentur AG 246b; Radharc Images 197tr; RBtravel 112tl; Ruslan Kudrin 176tl; Sasa Huzjak 258t; Sergey Kravchenko 37ca; Sergio Azenha 270bc; Stanca Sanda (iPad is a trademark of Apple Inc., registered in the U.S. and other countries) 176bc; Stock Connection 287bcr; tarczas 35cr; vitaly suprun 176cl; Wavebreak Media ltd 39cl, 174b, 175tr; **Allsport/Getty Images:** 238cl; **Alvey and Towers:** 209 acr, 215bcl, 215bcr, 241cr; **Peter Anderson:** 188cbr, 271br. **Anthony Blake Photo Library:** Charlie Stebbings 114cl; John Sims 114tcl; **Andyalte:** 98tl; **Arcaid:** John Edward Linden 301bl; Martine Hamilton Knight, Architects: Chapman Taylor Partners, 213cl; Richard Bryant 301br; **Argos:** 41tcl, 66cbl, 66cl, 66br, 66bcl, 69cl, 70bcl, 71t, 77tl, 269tc, 270tl; **Axiom:** Eitan Simanor 105bcr; Ian Cumming 104; Vicki Couchman 148cr; **Beken Of Cowes Ltd:** 215cbc; **Bosch:** 76tcr, 76tc, 76tcl; **Camera Press:** 38tr, 256t, 257cr; Barry J. Holmes 148tr; Jane Hanger 159cr; Mary Germanou 259bc; **Corbis:** 78b; Anna Clopet 247tr; Ariel Skelley / Blend Images 52l; Bettmann 181tl, 181br; Blue Jean Images 48bl; Bo Zauders 156t; Bob

Rowan 152bl; Bob Winsett 247cbl; Brian Bailey 247br; Chris Rainer 247ctl; Craig Aurness 215bl; David H.Wells 249cbr; Dennis Marsico 274bl; Dimitri Lundt 236bc; Duomo 211tl; Gail Mooney 277cctr; George Lepp 248c; Gerald Nowak 239b; Gunter Marx 248cr; Jack Hollingsworth 231bl; Jacqui Hurst 277cctr; James L. Amos 247bl, 191ctr, 220bcr; Jan Butchofsky 277cbc; Johnathan Blair 243cr; Jose F. Poblete 191br; Jose Luis Pelaez.Inc 153tc; Karl Weatherly 220bl, 247tcr; Kelly Mooney Photography 259tl; Kevin Fleming 249bc; Kevin R. Morris 105tr, 243tl, 243tc; Kim Sayer 249tcr; Lynn Goldsmith 258t; Macduff Everton 231bcl; Mark Gibson 249bl; Mark L. Stephenson 249tcl; Michael Pole 115tr; Michael S. Yamashita 247cctl; Mike King 247cbl; Neil Rabinowitz 214br; Pablo Corral 115bc; Paul A. Sounders 169br, 249ctcl; Paul J. Sutton 224c, 224br; Phil Schermeister 227b, 248tr; R. W Jones 309; Richard Morrell 189bc; Rick Doyle 241ctr; Robert Holmes 97br, 277ctc; Roger Ressmeyer 169tr; Russ Schleipman 229; The Purcell Team 211ctr; Vince Streano 194t; Wally McNamee 220br, 220bcl, 224bl; Wavebreak Media LTD 191bc; Yann Arhus-Bertrand 249tl; **Demetrio Carrasco / Dorling Kindersley (c) Herge / Les Editions Casterman:** 112ccl; **Dorling Kindersley:** Banbury Museum 35c; Five Napkin Burger 152t; **Dixons:** 270cl, 270cr, 270bl, 270bcl, 270bcr, 270ccr; **Dreamstime.com:** Alexander Podshivalov 179tr, 191cr; Alexxl66 268tl; Andersastphoto 176tc; Andrey Popov 191bl; Arne9001 190tl; Chaoss 26c; Designsstock 269cl; Monkey Business Images 26clb; Paul Michael Hughes 162tr; Serghei Starus 190bc; **Education Photos:** John Walmsley 26tl; **Empics Ltd:** Adam Day 236br; Andy Heading 243c; Steve White 249cbc; **Getty Images:** 48bcl, 100t, 114br, 154bl, 287tr; 94tr; David Leahy 162tl; Don Farrall / Digital Vision 176c; Ethan Miller 270bl; Inti St Clair 179bl; Liam Norris 188br; Sean Justice / Digital Vision 24br; **Dennis Gilbert:** 106tc; **Hulsta:** 70t; **Ideal Standard Ltd:** 72r; **The Image Bank/Getty Images:** 58; **Impact Photos:** Eliza Armstrong 115cr; Philip Achache 246t; **The Interior Archive:** Henry Wilson, Alfie's Market 114bl; Luke White, Architect: David Mikhail, 59tl; Simon Upton, Architect: Phillippe Starck, St Martins Lane Hotel 100bcr, 100br; **iStockphoto.com:** asterix0597 163tl; EdStock 190br; RichLegg 26bc; SorinVidis 27ctl; **Jason Hawkes Aerial Photography:** 216t; Duo M Johnson: 35r; **Kos Pictures Source:** 215cbl, 240tc, 240tr; David Williams 216b; **Lebrecht Collection:** Kate Mount 169bc; **MP Visual.com:** Mark Swallow 202t; **NASA:** 280cr, 280ccl, 281tl; **P&O Princess Cruises:** 214bl; **The Photographers' Library:** 186bl, 186bc, 186t; **Plain and Simple Kitchens:** 66t; **Powerstock Photolibrary:** 169tl, 256t, 287tc; **PunchStock:** Image Source 195tr; **Rail Images:** 208c, 208 cbl, 209br;

Red Consultancy: Odeon cinemas 257br; **Redferns:** 259br; Nigel Crane 259c; **Rex Features:** 106br, 259tc, 259tr, 259bl, 280b; Charles Ommaney 114tcr; J.F.F Whitehead 243cl; Patrick Barth 101tl; Patrick Frilet 189cbl; Scott Wiseman 287bl; **Royalty Free Images:** Getty Images/ Eyewire 154bl; **Science & Society Picture Library:** Science Museum 202b; **Science Photo Library:** IBM Research 190cla; NASA 281cr; **SuperStock:** Ingram Publishing 62; Juanma Aparicio / age fotostock 172t; Nordic Photos 269tl; **Skyscan:** 168t, 182c, 298; Quick UK Ltd 212; **Sony:** 268bc; **Robert Streeter:** 154br; **Neil Sutherland:** 82tr, 83tl, 90t, 118, 188ctr, 196tl, 196tr, 299cl, 299bl; **The Travel Library:** Stuart Black 264t; **Travelex:** 97cl; **Vauxhall:** Technik 198t, 199tl, 199tr, 199cl, 199cr, 199cctr, 199tcl, 199ctcr, 200, **View Pictures:** Dennis Gilbert, Architects: ADP Consulting, 106t; Dennis Gilbert, Chris Wilkinson Architects, 209tr; Peter Cook, Architects: Nicholas Crimshaw and partners, 208t; **Betty Walton:** 185br; **Colin Walton:** 2, 4, 7, 9, 10, 28, 42, 56, 92, 95c, 99tl, 99tcl, 102, 116, 120t, 138t, 146, 150t, 160, 170, 191cctcl, 192, 218, 252, 260br, 260l, 261tr; 261c; 261cr; 271cbl, 271cbr, 271ctl, 278, 287br, 302, 401.

DK PICTURE LIBRARY:
Akhil Bahkshi; Patrick Baldwin; Geoff Brightling; British Museum; John Bulmer; Andrew Butler; Joe Cornish; Brian Cosgrove; Andy Crawford and Kit Hougton; Philip Dowell; Alistair Duncan; Gables; Bob Gathany; Norman Hollands; Kew Gardens; Peter James Kindersley; Vladimir Kozlik; Sam Lloyd; London Northern Bus Company Ltd; Tracy Morgan; David Murray and Jules Selmes; Musée Vivant du Cheval, France; Museum of Broadcast Communications; Museum of Natural History; NASA; National History Museum; Norfolk Rural Life Museum; Stephen Oliver; RNLI; Royal Ballet School; Guy Ryecart; Science Museum; Neil Setchfield; Ross Simms and the Winchcombe Folk Police Museum; Singapore Symphony Orchestra; Smart Museum of Art; Tony Souter; Erik Svensson and Jeppe Wikstrom; Sam Tree of Keygrove Marketing Ltd; Barrie Watts; Alan Williams; Jerry Young.

Additional Photography by Colin Walton.

Colin Walton would like to thank:
A&A News, Uckfield; Abbey Music, Tunbridge Wells; Arena Mens Clothing, Tunbridge Wells; Burrells of Tunbridge Wells; Gary at Di Marco's; Jeremy's Home Store, Tunbridge Wells; Noakes of Tunbridge Wells; Ottakar's, Tunbridge Wells; Selby's of Uckfield; Sevenoaks Sound and Vision; Westfield, Royal Victoria Place, Tunbridge Wells.

All other images © Dorling Kindersley For further information see: www.dkimages.com